THE CHANGING
FACE OF POWER

THE CHANGING FACE OF POWER

BY CLAUDIA ALARCO ALARCO

NEW DEGREE PRESS

COPYRIGHT © 2020 CLAUDIA ALARCO ALARCO

THE CHANGING FACE OF POWER
ISBN   978-1-63676-526-6 *Paperback*
         978-1-63676-085-8 *Kindle Ebook*
         978-1-63676-086-5 *Ebook*

Para Flavia y Carlos—por ti y para ti
con todo mi amor.

CONTENTS

——

PROLOGUE

"Are they related?" I thought, squinting my eyes in a way that I would never do to the depreciating elasticity of my face today. To me, quite frankly, all of the faces looked the exact same.

In 2013, Alejandro Almaraz exhibited *Portraits of Power* at the Organization of American States' Art Museum of the Americas in Washington, D.C. I was seventeen at the time and had developed what I thought was a subtle yet painfully vivid infatuation with discovering inconspicuous gems in the area. I was on a mission, if you will. And the Art Museum of the Americas, tucked away between the Department of Interior and the Organization of American States, just a few steps away from the Washington Monument and the White House, proved to be exactly what I was looking for and *not* what I was ultimately hoping for.

This museum isn't the kind that screams "Come on in" or "Welcome, happy to have you" in a soft, butter-smooth toned voice. Instead, its outward appearance does the very opposite. Its chunky and awkward white walls make you think the actual voice of the structure is similar to the feeling of freshly cut nails against gravel.

The entrance was hard to find and its small size along with the chipping white paint on the outside makes you feel like you are in the wrong place. At seventeen, as you can imagine, this feeling isn't anything new, so I decided to go in anyway. What was the worst that could happen after all?

To my surprise, the eagle-eyed attendant was moderately welcoming and spoke about the collection that was currently in exhibit. I thanked him and took my first steps into the gallery. I remember it being cold. I remember it being eerily quiet—the kind of silence that forces you to show your vulnerabilities in the light of day.

I felt an imminent physical discomfort as I entered. I looked around and felt at a loss for words. Purely and utterly confused at what looked straight into me, or at least that's what it felt like. *Portraits of Power*, the exhibit that was on display, was a historic-photo mashup series of world leaders down the years, layered on top of each other.

It was daunting—Putin and Assad's faces melted into each other seamlessly. Margaret Thatcher's pearl necklace stood out like a sore thumb—a gentle, yet ferocious reminder of just how pervasive misogyny has been across cultures since the beginning of time.

At seventeen, I accepted what I saw. Today, I'm far from accepting the images of power that have been shoved so perniciously and delicately down my throat.

So, I ask you, what does power look like to you?

Does it look like the image reflecting back at you when you look in the mirror? What does it sound like, smell like, feel like? What kind of emotions does it trigger within?

Some might say that the image of power in their mind looks like the kind of image that you can find while strolling unabashedly through the halls of perhaps the National Gallery of Art in Washington, the Museum of Art in Philadelphia, or, in fact, any museum art collection around the globe. It might trigger feelings of distance, of longing, of something so perfect yet so unapologetically flawed you'll never be able to grasp.

Others say that the image of power in their mind is familiar, occupied by a sense of proximity, of certainty. Or they might say that it is occupied by a person whose power is imposing, filled with grandeur, rage, and might.

To me, the image of power in my mind is defined by a fervent sense of humility, of subtle yet brilliant virtue. The kind that doesn't yearn for your attention, it simply is. It doesn't require your validation, nor does it scream to catch a glimpse of your gaze. It simply whispers. Not with any overt desire for you to hear it, quite the contrary. It accepts that whether you hear it or not is not of their concern, it's yours.

The truth is this:

The conversations around power and the people who occupy it couldn't be more salient today. The United States is undergoing an unprecedented turning point in the history of this country. From a global pandemic that has killed more than

200,000 Americans and taken the lives of more than a million people worldwide, to a massive nationwide social unrest in the face of egregious killings of Black lives—this country will never be the same.

The unrest that began on the streets of Minneapolis has swelled into the largest public demonstrations for civil rights seen in generations. Hundreds of thousands of people are giving voice to the grief and anger that generations of Black Americans have suffered in the hands of a system that was inherently built to oppress.

Make no mistake, we are experiencing one of the most monumental periods of pain and rage due to the legacy and pervasiveness of racial violence, all while the COVID-19 pandemic is virtually laying bare all of America's structural inequalities.

As a non-Black Latinx person who has benefitted from a system built to uphold white supremacy and anti-Blackness both in Latin America and in the United States, I feel it is my responsibility to use this book and this platform to deconstruct, to educate, and to hopefully begin the conversations that we've been avoiding having for decades if not hundreds of years.

In writing this book, it has become very clear to me that we can't talk about Latinx power without talking about Black power.

We can't talk about #LatinxExcellence if we don't talk about the ways in which the concept of Latinx Excellence upholds and perpetuates anti-Blackness and white supremacy.

We can't talk about the rise of visibility in the Latinx community, if we don't talk about the ways in which we've continuously—time and time again—erased the lives of our Black Latinx brothers, sisters, and non-binary siblings by failing to see them as human, by failing to see them as our own.

We can't begin the work of dismantling, of unlearning, of deconstructing if we don't face the darkest parts of ourselves. We can't begin the work if we don't confront the times where we've failed to act, to speak, and to listen.

Without question, there have been times when we've stayed silent while our *abuelitas* told us to stay out of the sun, when we've heard our fathers say "he trabajado como negro," when we've failed to see our Latinidad in the faces and bodies of those of a darker hue.

To be frank with you, when I began this book, I came in with the idea that after years of being told that we weren't enough, that we were less than, that we were the "minority" that *this* would be my chance to fiercely and unapologetically rewrite the narrative. This would be my chance to scream from the highest mountains and showcase just how much power, excellence, and influence exists in the new generation of Latinx leaders today. I thought this would be the chance to write a book that solely focused on all the brilliant things we should be proud of.

Today, I stand corrected.

Through this book, and because of all the incredible people who have taken time out of their lives to be vulnerable with me, to challenge me, I know that we can't talk about our greatest victories without also discussing our greatest challenges that we face internally within the Latinx community.

So, I ask you: What does Latinx power look like to you?

If your definition of Latinx power and excellence doesn't include Black Latinxs, then you're not talking about Latinx power.

If your definition of Latinx power and excellence doesn't include Indigenous Latinxs, then you're not talking about Latinx power.

Latinx power, from its very inception, was built on the backs of Black and Indigenous people.

This book will discuss and showcase the victories, the excellence, the resilience of the new generation of Latinx leaders in the United States, *and it will also* confront the ingrained racism and anti-Blackness that has been passed down from generation to generation.

While courageously facing the darkest parts of ourselves and our history, I hope that this book will also bring you hope—certainly as much hope it has brought for me in my life.

AUTHOR'S NOTE

—

It was January 3, 2019 and the cold air made its way from my ankles slowly towards my thighs and then raced towards my chest. Delicately at first, and then overwhelming my senses all at once.

There's truly nothing that compares to the feeling of opening the car door to this particular destination, placing your feet on the ordinary yet extraordinary concrete and feeling as if all of your ancestors perniciously conspired for you to be just in this moment in time in this particular place on Earth.

Our car pulled up to the building right across from the US Capitol. I stood there—bare— in a soft light pink dress, nude heels, and a long black coat. It was swearing-in day and dozens of people lined up outside waiting to get through security. This day had been long-awaited by thousands all across the country. It was the culmination of ardent months in the making to elect the most diverse Congress in US history. Fifty-two percent of the incoming Democratic members of Congress were women, something that had never been thought possible before. And a record 103 women were elected to serve in the US House of Representatives—22 percent more than those who served in the previous 115th Congress. Five new women senators and ten incumbent women senators who were once again elected into office.[1]

Ostensibly an incredibly remarkable accomplishment on its own but even more than the representation of gender, it was a tremendous victory for those all over this nation that identified as Black and Brown. Thirty-four percent of incoming House Democrats identified as such. To make you swoon, the 116th Congress would also have more LGBTQ+ members than ever before with ten openly LGBTQ+ legislators to be sworn in that afternoon—two to the US Senate and eight to the US House of Representatives. This was the largest number of LGBTQ+ people to ever serve in either chamber. Half of those were women and two were people of color, up from just two LGBTQ+ women and one person of color in the previous Congress.[2]

I was twenty-three years old and had just graduated from Villanova University the previous spring. I had also just signed a lease on my very first apartment the month before and I was about five months into my very first job in the city that I always dreamed of working in. I didn't feel like I was underwater on Capitol Hill anymore, and things were really starting to feel like I was slowly but surely finding my place in the world.

---

1   Jennifer E. Manning, "Women in Congress: Statistics and Brief Overview," *Congressional Research Services* (January 2020): 2-10.

2   "Two LGBTQ Senators and Eight LGBTQ Representatives to Be Sworn In to Most Diverse Congress in U.S. History," Victory Institute, accessed September 13, 2020.

My job was far from anything I ever envisioned doing but it was also what I really needed at the time. I had a rather eclectic set of professional experiences before landing my first "big girl" job in Washington including experiences at the National Center for Children and Families, the National Institutes of Health, the US House of Representatives, and—most notably—the Obama White House. As a nineteen-year-old walking through the gates of the White House with an official badge around your neck, you don't fully comprehend the magnitude of the reality that you live—much less where these experiences would lead you.

Through my very first job, I ended up being exposed to a world that, frankly, I never even knew existed. Some imagine the industry of lobbying as a quintessential smoke-filled room with old cisgender, heterosexual white men oozing the patriarchy from their pores while bribing members of Congress to faithfully appease the power players in corporate America. And while some of that is still very much true today, it is not the whole truth.

At Villanova, and throughout my whole life in the United States, I had been in predominantly white institutions and spaces, but by the end of my college career I felt like I was missing something—something deep within myself. Something that connected me to *me* through my people, my language, and frankly who I had been until that point and who I wanted to become.

It was the kind of joy and fulfillment that I certainly didn't find during my day job at the lobbying firm, but on this day, I got just a taste of what I was seeking.

As soon as I made it through security, I could feel my body experiencing something different. My mouth was dry, my skin was moist, I could feel my chest pulsating as I walked by dozens and dozens of joyous beautiful brown faces—faces that actually looked like mine in those hallways for once—celebrating the realization of our ancestors' wildest dreams. The sounds, the voices, all caused me to feel my body escaping me. Time seemed to slow down—almost as if we were elegantly collecting B-roll. I couldn't believe it. There I was, sitting on the office couch of the newly sworn-in youngest member of Congress in US history, Congresswoman Alexandria Ocasio-Cortez—in complete and utter disbelief. Shocked at how I ever even got myself into this circumstance and beaming as I listened to stories in both Spanish and English as she walked into a room full of cheers and screams.

This was it. This was the start for me. For decades, members of the Latinx community had been undervalued, under-appreciated, underestimated—slaving away as the backbone of this country without an ounce of visibility or appreciation. But now, here we were. We were now in rooms, spaces, and institutions that were never created for us nor intended to include us. Nevertheless, there we were (and are)—taking up space, air, and power.

We are the soon-to-be new majority of this country and we are holding more power, visibility, and influence than we ever have before and it is just getting started. This triumph and evolution, though, is being met with violence and hatred. It's rampant, vile, and specifically targeted toward us. These despicable acts are a testament to the fact that power in this country is in fact changing and shifting with the Latinx

community at its forefront and the rest of America is starting to notice the inevitable change that is taking place on
all fronts of American society today. Folks in this country—from all walks of life—are starting to recognize that
potency. And they are beginning to realize that we are very
different from our parents, grandparents, and beyond. This
new Latinx generation, both Millennials and Gen Z'ers, are
forming a new identity, a new way of thinking, and a new
way of making change. We're proudly queer, Black, trans,
Indigenous, gender queer, hard of hearing, undocumented,
unafraid and we are rewriting our own narrative of what it
means to be *Latinx* in this country.

PART 1

EDUCATION

"I don't *give* advice to Millennials and Gen Z Latinos, I *get* advice from them."

- ANTONIO TIJERINO, CEO OF THE
HISPANIC HERITAGE FOUNDATION

We can all think back to a time that ignited a fire within our being. A time when we took a leap of faith with something we had never done before. And although we didn't quite know it at the time, it ended up being the start of something incredible, something you would've never even had the possibility to imagine.

When I first started thinking about the direction of this book, I knew that in order to encapsulate the power of Millennial and Gen Z Latinxs, I needed to grasp and showcase its very inception for each and every person.

Surely, none of these individuals became the disruptors, thought leaders, and agents of change without having that very first experience with the grandiosity and responsibility of power. What I find most remarkable about Millennial and Gen Z Latinxs in this journey is how early in their lives they've experienced these moments.

To us, as children of immigrants or immigrants ourselves, these circumstances shaped what would be our entire lives. As I listened to these stories, I couldn't help but to feel deeply moved and overcome with absolute admiration for the limitless *privilege* behind these circumstances.

Yes, *privilege*.

In understanding the privilege behind these circumstances, what I found most egregious about the largely accepted narrative that has been created around these instances in American culture is that it has cast a negative and undesirable light on these so-called "hardships".

I welcome you to challenge your own perspective and do away with the confines of viewing these experiences as "hardships" and rather see them for what they truly are: the beginning of an unveiling of the opportunity and potential to transform, influence, empower, and impact.

CHAPTER 1

MARISOL SAMAYOA

———

In 2010, in the midst of a deep nationwide recession, in the Los Angeles neighborhood of Boyle Heights, Marisol Samayoa embarked on a journey that led her to an unthinkable and unimaginable path toward change.

When I first spoke to Marisol in March 2020, I instantly felt that this person would be different than anyone else I interviewed. She had just finished serving as Deputy National Press Secretary for Pete Buttigieg's presidential campaign and there was just something about her. Her story made me feel so grateful to have had the pleasure of coming across her and made me feel so immeasurably excited to have a vessel to share her story.

I had never met Marisol before, but we did have a few mutual friends. She was warm and generous: made me feel welcome, which was something that up until that point no one had really transmitted so effectively the way that Marisol did.

I was, after all, a complete stranger to all of the people whose stories you see showcased in this book. And I made that decision purposefully. I trusted that this book would lead me to the people that I was truly meant to meet.

I still remember the jitters that I would feel when I looked at the clock and knew that it was time to physically pick up the phone and conduct an interview. I was so subtly and radiantly jumping straight out of my comfort zone. In the beginning, I had no idea what to expect. Here I was, a complete stranger who had come across their work and their story and had reached out to them to be a part of this. They didn't know who I was, where I came from, or how deeply I felt about this book. Yet, they agreed to hop on the phone with me and share a piece of themselves, share a piece of their story—even amid the COVID-19 global pandemic. That, to me, was and will forever be the most sacred gift I've received on this journey.

As I carefully listened to Marisol share her story with me, I felt moved by the way she described every single element of it. You could hear by the tone of her voice that recalling these details and re-opening these memories of her past moved her as much as it moved me.

Marisol was born and raised in one of Los Angeles's most historic and vibrant Latinx neighborhoods. Located East of the Los Angeles River and known for its bustling Latinx enclave, Boyle Heights provided Marisol an upbringing that was infused with a rich and omnipresent Mexican American heritage and a robust history of community activism.

Boyle Heights' beauty and richness are undeniable. The old brick workshops, soot-stained buildings, mesmerizing gilded murals, rumbling freeways, combined with the warmth of its people and the unrelenting desire for a better life makes Boyle Heights an unequaled enclave.

And while Boyle Heights' incomparable worth, value, and power stems from the resilience, cultural affluence, and strength in advocacy of its community members, it has also witnessed an unprecedented amount of under-investment from its local government.

With its long-standing history of community activism dating back to the Chicano movement in the 1960s, Boyle Heights is no stranger to fighting against racially unjust policies in regards to education, housing, urban development, transportation, and environmental health outcomes.

When Marisol was seventeen years old, she got a taste of just how important the fight for the improvement and advancement of her community would be.

From the moment she stepped foot in Woodrow Wilson High School, she began to get involved with InnerCity Struggle. InnerCity Struggle, founded in 1994, began when a small group of residents from Boyle Heights joined forces to find solutions in the face of a crisis of violence and crime in their community. With an overwhelming amount of neighborhood violence and crime at an all-time high, they refused to stand by idly. The founders decided to form an organization on the premise and spirit of the civil rights movement—one that fundamentally relied on the vision and service of its own residents for the development of a stronger Boyle Heights.[3]

It began with an investment in grassroots leadership. It began with the empowerment of progressive and powerful voices—both young and old. And most of all, it was rooted in the belief that every single person in Boyle Heights deserved for their community to be a stronger, equitable, and more thriving place.

Instead of seeking and investing in archaic, run-of-the-mill solutions, InnerCity Struggle opted for solutions that were forward-thinking, inclusive, and centered around the dignity and worth of every single community member.

Throughout their twenty-five-year history, they've empowered, trained, and developed thousands of leaders and Marisol Samayoa was one of them.

On June 22, 2010, Marisol was prepared to testify in front of the Board of Education of the City of Los Angeles as part of a concerted movement to advocate against incessant budget cuts present all throughout the high schools in the Eastside of Los Angeles.

In preparation for this day, Marisol along with a dozen other student organizers across the LA school system surveyed about 2,500 of their peers regarding their experiences with the impact of the decreasing investment and staff layoffs

---

3   "Our Story: 25 Years of Eastside Movement Building," InnerCity
     Struggle, accessed April 3, 2020.

in their schools. To make matters worse and intensify the need for community advocacy, there was also a lack of fully credentialed teachers and counselors—factors that greatly contributed to the pervasive difficulties in the schools.

InnerCity Struggle equipped their students with knowledge during after school programs and in-school learning sessions. Through the staff and student-led sessions, Marisol learned how to structure effective arguments, cater to your specific audience, how language impacts speech, etc. She was also educated on racism, classism, sexism, and colorism.

During the day, she was involved with InnerCity Struggle's flagship leadership program called United Students where she would be trained to become an expert community organizer through education, community building, and participation in direct action campaigns. Through this training, Marisol understood the history behind community organizing—from national to local movements. She knew that youth organizing was strategically focused on putting your solutions at the forefront of the public debate, and it was her hope that her testimony to the governing Board of Education would be just that.

The brightly lit board room accommodated around fifty people, with the school board members on one side and the students on the other. Once the majority of the audience had been seated, the board members began to enter the room.

Marisol remembers seven of them and one very important member in particular, the president of the board, Mónica García. Mónica was the only Latina on that side of the room and a familiar face to all of the students. She had previous involvement with the students and staff at InnerCity, and they were certain that they had an ally in her.

At 1:13 p.m., the meeting was called to order and the Pledge of Allegiance was recited promptly after.

After several action items were decided on by the board, it was finally time for the public to comment on the proposed budget for the following year.

Luckily for Marisol, she had time before she was scheduled to speak. Three adult advocates from several different organizations were scheduled to testify before her. She was scheduled to be the first student of five to address the board afterward.

Marisol, at seventeen, was taller than your average teenage girl. She was slim, and like most girls at that age, she carried herself with the slightest bit of awkwardness.

With her long black hair falling naturally to her waist, she tried to hide the white letters on her black short-sleeved shirt. It wasn't the shirt that the staff had hoped she would wear. All the students had decided on wearing a specific InnerCity Struggle branded shirt, and while she had all the intention of wearing it for the testimony that day, she simply forgot to wear it when she got ready that morning.

Marisol remembers the room being cold, much like what you'd expect from a government building. And it was unforgivingly quiet. The kind of quiet that you simply can't get away from, the kind that documents every single one of your moves and makes you feel overwhelmingly seen and heard in ways that you don't necessarily want to be.

Finally, it was Marisol's turn. She looked straight ahead at the fairly narrow walkway that she had to walk to get to the microphone and took one deep breath before taking the first step. At the end of the walkway, there was a single podium located at the center of the room connecting the board members to the public. It didn't seem extraordinarily long, but when Marisol actually had to make her way over, it seemed like the pathway would never end.

Once she arrived at the podium, all of the eyes in the room were on her. It was the kind of unforgiving gaze that makes you question your own ability to hold your own body and sustain your own skin.

Marisol grabbed her papers in her hands at the podium and began to address the members of the board. She could feel her voice shaking in waves— she fought them anyway.

"I want to make sure they remember," she thought to herself.

This wasn't the first time that Marisol was speaking in front of a large crowd. Marisol had practiced these remarks extensively and had even gotten her toes wet with musical theater in middle school. The audience, granted, was a bit different this time, but Marisol knew that a lot was at stake and took that very seriously.

While she gave her remarks, she began thinking about the moments that were the catalyst behind her why. Why was this important? Why was she there? Why this? And why now?

As she directed her words towards the board, her mind began to replay each and every one of the instances where the system had failed her.

The moments where Marisol would have to look into the eyes of a guidance counselor and her gaze was met with a look of disdain and dismissiveness when Marisol would mention which universities she was looking into.

The moments of unapologetic hesitation on behalf of the person who was supposed to be "invested" in her academic potential and future career.

The moments where Marisol would have to face the fact that this individual, who was supposed to be committed to her advancement and potential, *could not care less.*

"I don't know if that is going to help," the guidance counselor would say in a condescending tone.

These words Marisol would carry with her.

With the copious amounts of staff layoffs, Marisol's ability to make an appointment with her guidance counselor seemed almost an impossible task to achieve. A two- or three-month wait was expected and when she did finally have her appointment, she would be faced with indifference, dismissiveness, and unapologetic disdain.

However, the mere idea of having such vital resources diminished in such a way meant that students couldn't obtain the knowledge or the know-how of navigating the college admissions process was enough fuel to make this testimony worth it.

These budget decisions taken by these specific board members—who were so indubitably removed from the classrooms and students who had to face their impact—were taking an immense toll on the lives of thousands of students and their futures.

Once Marisol finished the last sentences of her remarks, the President of the Board Mónica García thanked her and the rest of the students for their testimony.

Marisol, relieved that her responsibilities and duties had now been taken care of, modestly ran to the back of the room as fast as she could.

The story doesn't quite end there. When I first listened to Marisol share this story with me, it was very clear that her beliefs and principles around change were stronger than ever: change doesn't come overnight, nor does it come by standing outside of a building and protesting.

"Change takes patience," she said to me during our very first call on a rainy afternoon in mid-March.

"Progress takes patience."

Years after this initial testimony, change did take place.

In February 2011, the Los Angeles Unified School Board of Education approved the opening of a new high school in a 5-2 favorable vote. And in the fall of that same year, when Marisol was a first-year student at the University of California, Long Beach, InnerCity Struggle invited her to visit and speak at the newly inaugurated Esteban E. Torres High School.

The high school, which sat on a 13-acre building framework, was equipped with brand new science laboratories, art classrooms, a robust library, an outdoor amphitheater, and an underground parking lot.

This was it. This was the beacon of hope that so many had fought for. This was a testament to the fact that community-driven ground-level organizing could bring about real, lasting, and equitable results.

For decades, the Eastside of Los Angeles had seen low-performing schools with devastating graduation rates, push-out rates, and low percentages of students who would later attend a four-year university.

To make matters worse, East Los Angeles only had one high school that served the community. It was originally built and structured to serve 1,500 students, yet at one point, it had more than 4,700 students enrolled. To accommodate such an overwhelming enrollment, the high school ran on a year-round academic calendar with students divided into three tracks, which resulted in each student losing seventeen academic school days *per year*.

However, the days of inaction were behind them.

A sign of hope and change was in the horizon, and it was now a palpable reality for Marisol.

It was a day that Marisol will never forget. As she walked into the halls of this new school, she could feel her body responding to this new reality. It was the brand-new squeaky-clean floor below her feet. It was the smell of brand-new textbooks giving off organic volatile compounds that so elegantly fused together produce a hint of the smell of vanilla. It was the distinct sensation that she felt gliding her fingers across the brand-new classroom desks.

"It was all so beautiful," she noted.

"It didn't feel like we were in Boyle Heights."

It was a reality that Marisol never imagined would come to fruition. It was a reality whose mere existence brought about such profound feelings of acceptance and to some degree, healing.

Healing and acceptance in the realization that she and so many others had been so utterly under-invested in. Healing and acceptance in the fact that this new generation of students would never have to experience that. This was progress—and it was possible. *Change was possible.* That elusive yet electrifying feeling when you know the community that you grew up in is moving forward, the community that you called home—is moving forward in the best way possible. New standards are being set and new horizons are being reached.

This high school was testament to what is possible when school and community leaders work together to create a beacon of hope and opportunity for students, their families, and their entire community.

CHAPTER 2

STEPHANIE OLARTE

In the spring of 2000, Stephanie Olarte attended an after-school program with Progreso Latino, a long-standing organization that serves Rhode Island's Latino and immigrant communities. This day would be the day that would spark the beginning of an indelible journey and career. Stephanie was thirteen years old at the time, and this event was a celebration of the culmination of a newly founded paid shadowing program that young Latinx leaders in the community took part in. The shadowing program, geared towards young teenagers, paired students with different professionals in the community from all different sectors in hopes of giving them a learning experience and preview into what a career in the respective sectors would look like.

Stephanie remembers feeling moderately excited for the event, but not particularly overcome with enthusiasm for it. As she walked in, she saw members of the staff and crew all judiciously preparing for the event. The event was expected to be attended by dozens of reporters from local news outlets as well as a handful of parents. The pressure was certainly palpable and Stephanie, for one, recalls feeling thankful that she didn't have to take part in the media ruckus. In Stephanie's thirteen-year-old mind, it wasn't *exactly* her strong suit.

Her close family friend who was also named Stephanie, on the other hand, was in the middle of it all. She had volunteered to be one of the students who was responsible for giving a speech on stage explaining how monumental the shadowing program was for her understanding of entering the workforce and all that came with it. Little did she know that a girl named Stephanie *would* deliver the speech, but that Stephanie would not be her.

With an hour left until the event, Stephanie Olarte sat down in the back of the rather large and daunting room alongside the staff responsible for putting this all together. The media had just begun to arrive and the parents of those who were scheduled to speak began to enter the room as well. As she looked on to the people piling in, Stephanie recalls starting to feel a little excited to see her friend, Stephanie, deliver a speech that she had been longing to deliver.

As she sat on a squeaky grey metal chair, she began to hear what sounded like her friend Stephanie crying at a distance. Then, she saw Stephanie's mother, Gloria, coming her way with a distinct, purposeful walk. Gloria was not only her best friend's mother, but she was her mother's best friend as well. This cannot be good, she thought to herself. Stephanie Olarte had known Stephanie's mother her entire life as the two young girls had always been friends. Gloria, who was supposed to be there for her daughter, approached Stephanie with a concerned expression on her face.

"Stephanie is really scared to go on stage," she began to say to Stephanie Olarte.

Stephanie paused, hoping she heard incorrectly and was not going to have to face what she thought Gloria would say next.

An awkward moment of silence endured.

Then, she dropped the bomb by saying, "I was hoping *you* could step up and do it."

Stephanie, fairly startled at this point, rushed to her friend. She found her friend in the girls' bathroom with her eyes swollen from crying and adults swarming around her. Stephanie had one mission when she approached her friend: do everything humanly possible to comfort her enough so she *wouldn't* have to go on stage and deliver that speech.

"You're so smart, Stephanie. You've taken so long to write this speech. I know you can do it."

"She's scared," Stephanie's mother interjected, almost defending her daughter.

Stephanie looked at her friend's mother in subtle disbelief and thought to herself, well she should've thought of that in the first place.

"There's no better person than you, Stephanie," the mother added in a calm and parental voice. One must note that she was referring to the Stephanie that *wasn't* her daughter.

In one second, Stephanie's plan for an uneventful day was ruined and she had no idea what this day would mean for what would be the rest of her life.

"I need to know now," said the director of the program with a preoccupied expression as they got closer and closer to the event's start time.

The weight was starting to mount on Stephanie's shoulders. She knew she needed to make a decision. And before the director could have an opportunity to continue to persuade or badger her, she ran towards the bathroom and locked the door.

It was then that a part of her knew that there was no way out of this one.

There was no convincing the other Stephanie that she should do it. There was no escape plan. It was, in fact, a "sí o sí" situation. For a moment, all she could think about was the fact that this wasn't *her* speech and it didn't seem fair to take this on. But she took one deep breath, looked straight at the reflection in front of her and decided to take it front and center.

When she came out of the bathroom, she had one goal in mind. If she had to get this done, then she needed it to be her own. So, she walked out of that small bathroom and got to work. Not leaving a single second for the adults in the room to say otherwise, she started memorizing Stephanie's old speech.

After some brief yet serious practice of her speech, Stephanie braced herself for the cameras, the crowd, and in a distant yet profoundly meaningful way—herself.

There was a crowd—and they surely made it known. Wearing a graceful pink long-sleeve shirt and a pair of dark purple corduroy jeans, she gathered in front of the microphone on stage. Stephanie had just gotten out of the wheelchair months before, and she was in the beginning phases of learning how to walk with her walker.

By this age, Stephanie had also become confident at setting her boundaries and communicating her needs as a disabled individual. She had no problem or difficulty in expressing to the staff and the adults responsible of any adjustments they needed to make in order for Stephanie to be safe and secure in that particular environment. She, at thirteen years old, asserted the kind of authority and grounds that grown adults only dream of asserting. And this authority and confidence in herself and her abilities were well-received by the adults that surrounded her.

Since there was hardly any space on stage for a walker, Stephanie supported herself by leaning on a wall that was beside the makeshift dark brown podium.

"Read what you read, but you are who you are," she recalls thinking to herself.

Once it was her turn to speak, she looked straight ahead to the main door in the back of the room—not paying too much attention to the lights and cameras that tempted her to get caught up in them.

While she fidgeted with the perspicuous fold in her paper, gliding her fingers back and forth, she came to an abrupt realization. Stephanie decided that she would ditch her friend's speech and simply speak from her heart.

When she spoke her first few sentences, she willfully adjusted her voice. She lowered it from the volume and pitch she initially started out with. She spoke about the perspective of what it meant to be invested in, professionally, at such a young age.

Solemn silence—milliseconds of mere despair between inanimate eyes and grappling silence—and glares from the people gathered in front of her.

Her speech was now over, and it was time for the dreaded question-and-answer segment of the event. Two police officers volunteered to ask her questions and Stephanie answered them with ease.

"Now, just walk away," Stephanie told herself.

"I did this without any preparation, and I did good!" she remembers thinking.

As soon as Stephanie exited the stage, people swarmed her to congratulate her.

When it all set in, she remembered that her own mother wasn't there to witness it. This was certainly no fault of her own, as there was no way that she would have known when she dropped Stephanie off that morning that her daughter would be given the opportunity to speak at the event. So, as soon as she hopped into her mother's car at the end of that day, she told her everything.

"Y cómo te fue?" her mother, Nancy, asked.

"Súper bien, no dije lo que preparó Stephanie."

And it would be seventeen years later that Stephanie would have the opportunity to do the same and her mother would be right by her side.

Almost two decades after this opportunity, Stephanie, who is now in her thirties, was asked to speak in front of hundreds, not by accident and with a real podium this time.

Stephanie's alma mater, the University of Rhode Island, asked her to be a keynote speaker for an event that celebrated the excellence and the achievements of Black and Brown female scholars.

Stephanie was asked to speak on the empowerment of women, the connection between these achievements, and the prevalence and need for the recognition of intersectionality.

Stephanie, a proud Latina and disabled individual, was truly the perfect person for the job.

For this event, Stephanie had *weeks* to prepare. She practiced and practiced endlessly for days using her sister, Jalissa, as an audience or second ear to the speech. On the day of the event, Stephanie's mother drove her to the reception where Stephanie would be speaking. Determined to make her mother feel as comfortable as possible at the event, she made sure to translate—in real time—so Stephanie's mother knew exactly what was happening. Like so many of us, Stephanie experienced that fleeting worry that because our parents don't speak the language, they won't feel included or won't understand what's going on around them.

You know the feeling.

When you're desperately translating as fast as humanly possible just so there's not a single second that your parents feel or are made to feel like outsiders, working your mind past the limitations that you once thought you had.

Stephanie, with this in mind, made sure her mom felt comfortable and included in the environment at the reception before she had to leave to give her remarks.

"I took a whole week to write, edit, and learn this speech," she said to her audience in the elegantly lit ballroom.

"But somehow I feel like I don't need to use it," she continued.

Two seconds later, Stephanie had left the podium and started talking *to* the audience and not *at* the audience.

She walked right through to them, without an ounce of hesitation. She walked through those tables and rows of people like she was born to be doing this exact thing in this exact moment in time. You know that feeling when you know you're doing something really, really well? And it's this mutual understanding with the universe that you're right where you're supposed to be? This was it. Stephanie, in front of an entire ballroom of Black and Brown women, was exactly where *she* was meant to be.

"I should do this more often," Stephanie thought to herself as she felt the energy and connection with the people in that room.

In the middle of the applause and excitement from the crowd when she finished her speech, Stephanie took one good look at her mother.

It didn't matter that the whole room gave her a standing ovation, the only person she cared to look at was su mamá. It was a sight that she'll never forget.

Her mother, Nancy, sat there stoically with her eyes welled up with tears in complete and utter awe of the emotion that her daughter had created for everyone in that room.

It was rare for Stephanie to ever see her mother cry, but this sight of her daughter was the true exception.

Even without her mother understanding a word of the English that her daughter had spoken in her speech, she knew that her daughter had done something remarkable. She didn't need to understand every word that she said because all she needed was to see the expression on her daughter's face—an expression of certainty, of wisdom, of confidence in her own ability to transcend, to reach, and to move. It was in this moment that she knew that all the sacrifices, todas las adversidades, were worth it.

Stephanie walked back to her mother's table to see her face wearing the biggest, most radiant smile.

"¿Te gusto?" Stephanie asked.

"Sí! ¿Que dijiste?" Stephanie's mother said with undeniable excitement.

"No fue lo que escribí," Stephanie answered telling her mom that she had gone completely off script—yet again.

"Oh my god que bueno," her mother celebrated.

"Mamá, y no me dio pena!" Stephanie said to her mother with pride.

"Ni pena ni que nada. "

In that moment, Stephanie knew that in a room full of exceptional women, she wasn't the exception—she was the rule. They were all the rule, including her mother. Excellence was the rule.

CHAPTER 3

ALEJANDRO BARRAGÁN

In September 2008, in the cafeteria of St. John Bosco Elementary School on the west side of San Antonio, Texas, Alejandro Barragán met one of the most well-respected leaders of his community—a man that unbeknownst to him, at the tender age of twelve, would become a tremendous part of his personal and professional career.

Alejandro grew up on the west side of San Antonio surrounded by a remarkable community of people who not only looked like him but represented him as well. There was no shortage of exemplary leaders on the local, city, and state level, who made his community a nourishing place to grow up.

Alejandro, a fifth grader at the time, didn't know what to expect when he got the news that then-state representative, Joaquin Castro, was going to visit his local boy scout troop.

The troop meetings, which would take place every Tuesday evening at 7 p.m., were routinely attended by their scout master and, at most, a couple of parents. This time, though, things were quite different.

There wasn't a single parent that was not in attendance in that small elementary school cafeteria that night. Alejandro and the rest of his troop were fully aware of this exception and started to get the feeling that this meeting was of great importance—something that the parents clearly did not want to miss.

Routinely, before the meetings would begin, the troop would congregate outside of the cafeteria. The boys, who were huddled up, looked out through the open doors in front of the building and into the parking lot.

There he was—Joaquin Castro.

His walk, his purposeful and powerful walk, would be the inevitable giveaway to the troop that this was the person that they had been expecting. Alejandro remembers this walk fondly.

Deliberate. Strong-willed. Powerful.

Unbeknownst to Alejandro, this would be the first of many times that he would witness that exact walk.

In that moment, as he admired Joaquin Castro walking into the building, the troop started whispering amongst themselves.

"That has got to be him," one said.

"Do you think that's him?"

"That's definitely him," another responded.

In hindsight, Alejandro remembers that these whispers weren't so discrete as the troop had imagined them to be at the time. That detail that comes to him with a great amount of warmth today.

Joaquin Castro, and the staffer that accompanied him that night, walked right into the cafeteria. The room took notice.

Joaquin wore a gold tie and a navy suit, Alejandro recalls.

There was no podium, but the cafeteria table setup did the trick.

The troop sat facing Castro, attentively and in awe while he was introduced by the scout master. What came after this, Alejandro remembers with a great deal of respect and vivid emotion.

Then-state representative Castro spoke about his experience of leaving his hometown of San Antonio to pursue his undergraduate education at Stanford University and later at Harvard Law. He also candidly talked about his immense desire to come back to his community, back to his home.

Comments like these were hard to come by in Alejandro's community of West San Antonio. Most folks in town had the belief that in order to become someone, to do something meaningful in the world, one needed to leave San Antonio— leave it behind for good.

This was the first time that Alejandro heard someone share the beliefs that deep down inside he knew he had too. And it wasn't just anybody who shared these beliefs with him. It was someone who had earned the respect and admiration of so many in his community.

It was someone who had gone on to achieve such incredible things, such unimaginable things.

Little did Alejandro know that more than a decade later, he would not only have the pleasure of working for one Castro, but both. Alejandro's first job out of college was working for Joaquin Castro on his Congressional re-election campaign before joining Julián's presidential campaign.

The Castro brothers are the kind of Latinx political dream duo that America never saw coming. Joaquin and Julián are identical twins who hail from an incredibly well-respected, politically active Mexican American family in San Antonio, Texas. Both graduates from Stanford University and Harvard Law School as well as products of the public-school system on the west side of San Antonio, they have been absolutely monumental in their contributions to the state of American politics.

Joaquin Castro has served as US Congressman for the 20th District of Texas since 2013 and formerly served as State Representative representing Texas's 125th House District.

Julián, on the other hand, served his hometown of San Antonio on City Council as the youngest city councilmember in history at age twenty-six and went on to be elected as mayor in 2009, becoming the youngest mayor of a top-fifty American city. A year into his term as mayor, he was named to the World Economic Forum's Young Global Leaders and Time Magazine's 40 under 40 list of rising stars in American politics.[4]

Julián later gained national attention when he delivered the keynote address at the Democratic National Convention in 2012, becoming the first ever Latinx to do so. Two years later, he accepted President Barack Obama's offer to join his administration and served as the United States Secretary of Housing and Urban Development and had a remarkable number of accomplishments during his term as secretary including stabilizing the US housing market, rebuilding communities that had been affected by natural disasters through a $1 billion Natural Disaster Resilience Fund, as well as expanding the lead safety protections in federally assisted housing across the nation.[5]

Julián Castro's solid record of executive experience put him on the map to be considered a formidable contender for the presidency and a national leader in a prime position to be the game-changing figure capable of pushing Latinx voter turnout to record high levels.

Many years after Alejandro's encounter in that elementary school cafeteria at age twelve, Alejandro—now a full-fledged young professional—was brought on board to work on Julián Castro's 2020 presidential campaign.

---

4   "Julián Castro," U.S. Department of Housing and Urban Development, accessed July 22, 2020.

5   "Exit Memo: Department of Housing and Urban Development," Obama White House Archives, accessed July 29, 2020.

So, on January 12, 2019 in Guadalupe Plaza on the west side of San Antonio, Alejandro stood serenely behind the crowds alongside other campaign staffers when one of them tapped his shoulder to grab his attention.

"Check this out," he said.

Alejandro was familiar with parts of the speech that were scheduled to be given that day because weeks prior to this official announcement, he had heard Julián Castro practice bits and pieces here and there.

He thought he'd known, for the most part, everything that was to be expected. And he did, until Julián started speaking in Spanish.

The ability or inability to speak Spanish is an incredibly sensitive and complex issue in the Latinx community in the United States. For hundreds of thousands of second-generation, third-generation Latinxs who grew up in a time where speaking English was vehemently required by all, it's no surprise that they don't have a fluency in the language.

For immigrant generations like myself who immigrated in the early 2000s, my ability to speak, to read, to live in my native tongue has always been ingrained in me as an unequivocal asset.

The truth is this: Your ability or inability to speak Spanish does not make you more or less authentically Latinx in the United States. It is not the *only* variable that makes somebody authentically Latinx, but it is a part of the overall connection to the Latinx community.

So, when Julián Castro gave his speech in both English and Spanish, he made history and touched millions across this country.

"Cuando mi abuela llegó aquí hace ya casi 100 años, estoy seguro que nunca se imaginó que sólo dos generaciones después, unos de sus nietos formaría parte del Congreso de los Estados Unidos y que el otro estaría ante ustedes— hoy—diciendo las siguientes palabras—yo soy candidato para la Presidencia de los Estados Unidos."

"When my grandmother got here almost 100 years ago, I'm sure that she never could have imagined that just two generations later—one of her grandsons would be serving as a member of the United States Congress and the other would be standing with you here today to say these words—I am a candidate for President of the United States of America."

As soon as Alejandro heard these words, these powerful words, uttered in Spanish he couldn't help but to think of that twelve year old bright-eyed kid in that elementary school cafeteria. In the community that gave him everything and with the people that made it all possible for him to be where he is today, this was the moment. He proudly stood holding an indomitable hope and vision not only for this community, but for communities all over this nation.

CHAPTER 4

PAULINA MONTAÑEZ-MONTES

For so many of us who have immigrated or experienced secondhand immigration, we know exactly what it feels like to ask this country for something that we need. It doesn't matter how small it may be. For anyone who has been made to feel that they owe something to this country for even being here, it can feel enormous. It can feel like the kind of weight that you are too afraid to weigh in the first place.

In 2005, when Paulina Montañez-Montes was just sixteen years old, she followed her mother into an elementary school cafeteria in her hometown of Sacramento, California.

The school, which happened to be Paulina's former elementary school, was just around the corner from their house. It was a school night and Paulina had just gotten home when her mother approached her with what felt like a seemingly innocuous request to accompany her to the local townhall.

However, it was anything but innocuous. And it was certainly a night that she would never forget.

For months, Paulina's mother had been struggling to get a neighbor to trim or remove a tree which had been blocking the family's driveway. She reached out to the neighbor to try to come to an agreement. Promises were certainly made but time after time, nothing would change.

For many, this might seem like an insignificant inconvenience but for Paulina's mother it was a different reality. It was an injustice and a disservice that she wasn't willing to put up with any longer.

And rightly so.

As immigrants, as women, as people who stand on land that isn't their own—we're not taught to ask for what we need.

So, when Paulina's mother asked for her daughter to accompany her, both Paulina and her mother knew that it wasn't just to have her daughter by her side—it was more than that. Much more.

Paulina knew that she needed to translate her mother's grievances. She was a teenager, and, by that point, she had been translating for her parents for years.

This time, though, things were different.

She felt somewhat annoyed and embarrassed for being put in this situation. When she walked into the large cafeteria and saw rows of people sitting and waiting for the event to start, she could feel the discomfort and embarrassment starting to form inside of her.

But she also knew that her mother deserved what she was owed.

She remembered that time and time again, Paulina's mother told her that it didn't have to be this way—and that people had the right to know.

Her mother just wanted for *someone* to know. The family paid taxes like anyone else in that room and they deserved fair and equal representation before their elected officials. They deserved acknowledgement, at the very least.

The town hall officially began, and folks began to form a line to be called on and speak. Paulina's mother walked firmly towards the line and stood near the second row from the front. As the line advanced, Paulina's nerves began to mount.

They were more than nerves, though. There was a sense of fear and protectiveness over her mother.

We've all experienced it one way or another. The kind of protectiveness that we experience when we rush to repeat what our parents ordered at the restaurant because we can't possibly allow room for the waiter to ask them to repeat themselves and make them feel less than, make them feel like we or they don't belong.

The hurricane of feelings we get in the seconds our parents say something to the teacher, to the neighbor—the attention is certainly on them but in some light-reflecting way it feels as though it's on us. It feels as though every word uttered is there for us to run, to catch, and to carry.

Our parents need protecting is what it feels like. What a strange sentiment. Parents are for protecting children, aren't they? Yet for every interaction our parents have with the English-speaking world—it seems as though *we* hold the capes. We do the protecting, no matter what the circumstance. No matter how small our bodies might be, we fit into whatever form is needed from us.

And they ask us how advocacy comes so naturally to us. How did we become so good at standing up for ourselves you ask? Did *you* not grow up entirely having to defend your existence? We've not only had to stand up for ourselves, but we've had to stand up for those who we love. We know it's out of necessity and we know we don't have a choice, but oftentimes it comes wrapped in a confluence of mixed feelings. Paulina had *all* the feelings, and all at once.

As they began to get closer and closer to the microphone, she—like any other teenager—felt overwhelmingly annoyed to have to be in a space in front of so many people with her mother. It was the pinnacle of embarrassment on so many different levels.

The time had come, and it was now their turn to approach the front of the line.

Paulina's mother approached the front of the line as though she had done it a thousand times in the past, with confidence and calm. Paulina followed.

Paulina's mother looked at Paulina nodding for her to begin to speak.

Sus palabras llenas de valor y certeza, explaining what had been happening to her and her family.

Paulina looked up at the councilmember, who stood at six-foot-something, as he listened attentively to her mother with ease.

Paulina spoke the words directing them to the councilmember and his staffers, her cheeks hot from the nerves with subtle hesitation.

"How do people even do this, what do I do with my hands?" she remembers thinking to herself.

With one deep moment of reflection, she looked into her mother's eyes, and she kept speaking. Subtly shaking, she continued one word after the other.

After Paulina finished speaking, she quickly sat down. Her mother followed.

Then, came the unexpected twist that no one could have expected.

After the town hall meeting, Councilmember Kevin McCarty thanked them both for their remarks and subtly yet not subtly began to respond in fluent Spanish.

Imagine the shock.

Suddenly, Paulina was overwhelmed with relief. It didn't all fall on her shoulders and her mother would be able to speak for herself.

That sixteen year old girl just a few years later would graduate from the University of California, San Diego, then continue to get her master's degree from the George Washington University, later on spending nearly a decade serving as an advisor and operative in both local and federal government and on campaigns.

She would even go on to serve this same councilmember—en español y en inglés.

CHAPTER 5

EDGAR GONZALEZ JR.

———

At the end of the spring 2016, Edgar Gonzalez Jr. returned home from his first year at Harvard University. His year was full of ups and downs, but for Edgar, being home came with a set of emotions that he certainly never expected to feel.

For many college students, coming home after the first year of college is fairly unsettling. After enjoying a year full of independence and autonomy, students return to a place where they do not enjoy the same privileges. They realize that the independence they once felt is being suppressed by a parent's desire to once again parent, care for, and protect. Parents are able to dictate what they are able to do and when they are able to do it. In the process, soon-to-be second year college students will yearn for a taste of that freedom again—the freedom they've now realized they value, the freedom they've now come to love.

While a mixture of these feelings is true for some students, it certainly wasn't the case for Edgar. Edgar's discovered feelings and realizations about life back home in La Villita and, in contrast, life at Harvard were far beyond what other nineteen-year-olds have to come to terms with.

To say that life in La Villita in the South Side of Chicago to life in Cambridge, Massachusetts was a cultural adjustment would be a gross understatement. La Villita, where Edgar grew up, is a thriving Mexican American enclave dubbed "the Mexico of the Midwest". The taquerias, panaderias, tortillerias could fool just about anyone for a street in América Latina. While La Villita is a heavily under-invested and under-resourced community, there was anything but a lack of belongingness and unity amongst its members.

La Villita, for better or for worse, is also a place where violence, to some degree, prevails. The gunshots heard at night don't surprise anyone in the neighborhood as they happen quite often. Edgar, in many ways, had come to accept this reality. Not from a sense of complacency but rather from a sense of "matter of fact". He, and so many others in the community, have grown to accept this harsh reality that came with living in La Villita. The reality of being a part of it meant that you needed to come to an understanding that you either did well, got an education, and started a career or you were going to end up dead. It's a mentality that everyone embraced, willingly or otherwise.

Edgar ostensibly grew up with a unique understanding that he needed to rise above because the alternative would have to be facing the brash reality of life in a gang, in jail, or—most tragically —death. It was as simple as that.

Edgar in fact rose above it all and was able to make it to the world's most prestigious academic institution, Harvard. Life at Harvard, as you can imagine, surely presented its challenges. Its perfectly coiffed grassy lawns, boundless privilege, and the life that came with being a part of such an elite institution were really difficult adjustments for Edgar. The bustling Harvard Square neighborhood, local ambiance-obsessed coffee shops, New England autumns, and the pervasive elitist culture were incredibly disorienting. However, the real and raw moments were in the subtleties. The silent nights were rather startling for Edgar.

In La Villita, Edgar had been accustomed to falling asleep to anything but silence. The sounds of gunshots, the yells, screams, the screeches of cars racing had grown to be familiar to him, comforting in a way. They felt like home. But at Harvard, there were hardly any noises at night that made Edgar feel *safe*. The lack of noises and sounds—the silence was crippling and unsettling for him.

One night while walking back to the Harvard campus from a local party at MIT at 4 a.m., Edgar couldn't believe his eyes, but he couldn't believe his ears either. It was 4 a.m. in Cambridge and there were absolutely no cops to be found anywhere. Not a single person in the streets. As Edgar kept incessantly turning around looking for the police or just *someone*, he grappled with a feeling that had a minuscule taste of safety. Did he feel safe? Why would this make him feel safe? This was far from anything he had known to be normal when he was at home in Chicago. Had his concept of safety shifted so drastically?

More feelings like this began to emerge and they had gotten to Edgar. He couldn't stand being away from his family—his parents, his sister, his home. He had difficulty concentrating in his coursework and longed for the day that he was back in Chicago—finally at home. However, when that day came it was far from anything that he had imagined it would be.

It was the spring of 2016, and Edgar had finally crossed the finish line in his first year at Harvard. He was back home in La Villita and eager for a sense of normalcy and comfort. At this point, Edgar had been home for a week when his father approached him.

"Te acuerdas del güey que vivía enfrente," referring to the neighbor in the house across the street from them.

Edgar nodded yes, as he remembered exactly who his father was referring to.

"Lo tronaron en la esquina" his father added. Tronaron, in this case, means killed.

The man whom Edgar's father was referring to was shot. Over the course of a few weeks, five other people had gotten shot as well within a two to three block radius from his house. Edgar quickly opened up the community's Facebook page which usually reported incidents before the Chicago Tribune or the local Telemundo station. It was the trusted source for the community. When he opened the page, he found the confirmation that he was looking for.

It was true. People in the neighborhood corroborated posts that people had made about the shootout. He found comments of people recounting how many bullets they heard.

One thought came to Edgar's mind. It was a resounding sense of guilt and rabid frustration. He knew that those who got shot and killed that night, could have been anyone. It could've been him for all he knew. It could have been his sister or his parents. Edgar had been in very similar conversations to this one with his father and recalls having countless experiences like this before, where he heard of violence and death just feet away from his home. It wasn't anything new. But this time, these deaths evoked a new realization and a new set of emotions within him.

While wrestling with feelings of anger and hurt, hurt for the pain of those lost in his community, he found himself facing the realization that, for so many years, he and the rest of his community had been normalizing violence. He felt a jolt inside him. As he confronted these thoughts in deep and somber silence, memories of his own family and neighbors saying, "two to three got shot—not as bad as last week," or things that he had said in response to this pervasive violence. He remembered asking his mom why they didn't buy bulletproof windows for their house when he was younger. He recalls his mother's response, the feeling of helplessness from a parent who feels in part a sense of failure when she told him that they just couldn't afford it. And that was that.

These feelings caused a storm within him. Was this complacency? Complacency to violence? He knew it wasn't that. This was simply *survival*. This was the only way people knew how to confront this reality, their reality. In this deep thought, he remembers saying to himself "esto no puede seguir así."

This cannot go on.

In that moment, he knew that the only thing that could help heal from the normalization of violence would be action. He returned to Harvard that following fall knowing that he had one goal in mind: to use all the resources and opportunities at his disposal at Harvard to be able to bring that talent back home and make the difference that he knew he could make.

So, after graduating from Harvard, on a cold Friday evening in January of 2020 just a few years later in Chicago, Edgar became one of the youngest lawmakers to ever serve in the Illinois State Legislature.

Since that transformative night in his hometown, Edgar has embodied the kind of leadership that is at the forefront of the multi-generational progressive movement in Chicago— focusing on fighting for a living wage, affordable healthcare and housing, and a tax system that works for working families like his own and in all of its humble glory becoming the new face of power in Springfield, Illinois.

PART 2

VOICE

"It has been so important for me to embrace what I personally bring to the table. Let your stories inform your voice."
- VIVIAN NUÑEZ, FOUNDER OF TOO DAMN YOUNG

The young Latinx voice in the United States is so distinct. Its powerful authenticity, its irrefutable might, its ability to connect and to persuade, to be completely unapologetic, and its unassailable way that it transcends generations—it represents the peak of the collective fight of all our ancestors on these very lands and far, far away.

In these stories, there also lies a truth unlike any other. And it has something to do with this:

When Millennial and Gen Z Latinxs start amplifying their voices—no matter what the circumstance—it not only changes them as people, but it also fundamentally changes the community and society that surrounds them.

CHAPTER 6

JONATHAN FLORES

———

Jonathan Flores was seventeen years old when he made the resolute commitment to serve and defend his country against all enemies foreign and domestic. He had no idea what his journey would have in store for him after committing to serve in this capacity, but he certainly could never have imagined the unprecedented impact that this decision in joining the US Army would have on the trajectory of his life.

After successfully completing ten weeks of basic combat training, as well as an additional thirteen weeks of advanced individual training that involved language, negotiations, and regional training, Jonathan was deployed to Afghanistan and chosen to serve on the ground as a Civil affairs specialist.

Civil affairs specialists are the public relations officials who work with civilian and military liaisons to ensure the safety of both soldiers and civilians, as well as the success of the military operations as a whole. This role, coveted by many in the Army, also focuses on fostering and maintaining communication with civilians on the ground as well as civilian aid agencies.

Essentially, civil affairs specialists were required to be culture experts and use critical thinking, civil analysis, negotiation, and mediation techniques to prevent or solve an issue on the ground. This role was typically given to more senior members so the fact that Jonathan, a recent high school graduate, had earned it meant that he presented a skill set and talent that was yearned by many.

By the start of the summer of 2010, Jonathan had already spent six months traveling the country of Afghanistan and building the relationships that were necessary to be effective in his role. In fact, he had been specifically deployed to a village in the Shah Wali Kot district in Southeast Afghanistan where Taliban activity was known to be rising and gaining momentum. That year, in particular, was the height of international military efforts in Afghanistan with just over 100,000 US troops on the ground and around 40,000 troops from fifty other nations. Yet despite the compelling military presence, the Taliban was still to be defeated.[6]

Over the years, the lack of success in defeating the Taliban has been blamed on the failings of Western leadership and strategy, on the hubris and incoherence of the international effort, and on flaws in counterinsurgency tactics and operations.[7] As for the brave men and women who were on the ground, none of this was common knowledge. They did

---

6   Theo Farrell "Unbeatable: Social Resources, Military Adaptation, and the Afghan Taliban." *Texas National Security Review* 1, no. 3 (May 2018): 59-60.

7   Theo Farrell "Unbeatable: Social Resources, Military Adaptation, and the Afghan Taliban." *Texas National Security Review* 1, no. 3 (May 2018):60-61.

what they were asked to do in the name of defending the US Constitution and Jonathan was not going to be the one to question it.

His mission was clear. He was responsible for being a representative of the US Army and building trusting relationships with locals on the ground. This was very important to Jonathan because he believed that beyond the strict set of responsibilities that he had as a civil affairs specialist, a huge part of his role was to listen and try to understand how the Afghan people were feeling, what perceptions they had of the US involvement on the ground in their home country, and what concerns they had with their own government.

One day, a small team of four including Jonathan set out to visit a relatively small community in the area. The entire area was the size of multiple communes and it was an extremely hot summer day. Jonathan and his team were wearing approximately seventy pounds worth of gear: gloves, boots, uniform, two weapons, ammunition, and body armor. Not an easy task, even for men and women of their preparedness and stature.

These visits, as Jonathan remembers them, were not just about doing their job, but also about worrying and looking out for one's own safety and the well-being of your colleagues. It was no secret to anybody that day that they were in a high-danger zone and that they needed to act accordingly.

The people they often came in contact with were people who lived in these villages and in these communities for centuries, folks with longstanding ties that transcended generations.

Americans, in this case, were the ones who were foreigners entering these spaces and communities with guns and interpreters. And, at least for Jonathan, there was a huge desire to learn, to listen, and to understand.

As civil affairs specialists in this area, it was their duty to persuade local leaders to attend town halls that took place every month. It was the only way to engage and involve people in the conversations around the Afghanistan that *they* wanted and needed.

As one can imagine, persuading locals to attend these meetings was incredibly difficult and tumultuous. After being confronted with several zealous no's that day, the team was feeling discouraged and frustrated. They felt as though they were the only ones who were making efforts to try to better the country as a whole but the Afghan people didn't seem to have an interest in the betterment of their own country or, more specifically, the route that their country would take *after* the United States left.

With all of the no's that they encountered, it was difficult for Jonathan to grasp the reality behind the rejection that him and his team were facing. As the son of a single mother and a person who grew up in poverty, Jonathan never really had the privilege of saying no. He knew what it meant to feel powerless. Yet he couldn't fathom the fact that the people in the village rejected the opportunity to hold power over their own destiny, over their own country and future.

As he continued walking and trying to make sense of the situation, he carefully observed his surroundings. Kids were playing around barefoot, older men walking were looking at them with anything but ease, and the mud huts surrounding the perimeter were disarming. The dry heat was especially unbearable.

Suddenly, in the middle of the path, Jonathan made eye contact with someone who seemed familiar.

He was a man—a young man—who stood about 5-foot-9 and approximately fifteen-feet away from Jonathan's unit. His face was burnt from what seemed to be so much exposure to the sun and his teeth were visibly deteriorating. This, unfortunately, wasn't entirely uncommon for people in the region. He wore loose fitting pants and a traditional Afghan robe.

Jonathan specifically noted that this man was fairly young, which indicated that he was potentially a possible threat due to the Taliban's interest in recruiting young men for their forces.

"He thinks you're Afghan," said the interpreter who was standing beside Jonathan. The young man had asked if Jonathan was Afghan.

"No, I don't speak Farsi," Jonathan said facing the young man with a smile.

"We have very similar skin color," the young man said to Jonathan in Farsi.

Jonathan looked down at his own skin and then moved his gaze over to the skin of the young man. He laughed warmly as he realized that the young man had thought that Jonathan was an Afghan interpreter. After all, the interpreters had no way of outwardly differentiating themselves from the rest of the unit.

As they mutually came to an unspoken understanding that they would continue the conversation, the young man began squatting down. Jonathan willingly followed.

"What's going on," the interpreter for the unit said to Jonathan.

Jonathan didn't respond.

He proceeded to take his helmet and his gloves off. With each item that he took off, he began to create waves of trust around them. His superiors *hated* when he did that. They were, after all, in a *war zone*. But Jonathan understood that if he ever wanted to have an authentic egalitarian conversation with someone from the community, then he needed to show that he was worthy of trust. He needed to earn it.

So, with that in mind, he took his weapon off of him and firmly placed it on the ground between them.

The young man showed amusement and excitement with a hint of admiration for the weapon.

A young boy who was made responsible for attending to the village, suddenly approached them to bring them chai on a strikingly elegant tray of sugar cubes.

The young man gestured that they drink the tea. Jonathan happily joined him.

This moment set off a rocket of thoughts bursting in Jonathan's mind. Here he was—fresh out of high school—in a literal *war zone* where he was inculcated to view everyone around him as enemies. Yet, here he was drinking tea and being human alongside a complete stranger—someone who could have easily been incredibly dangerous, but Jonathan decided to take a chance.

The men in Jonathan's unit formed a circle around them and faced outward to protect them from anything that could ensue. This heightened the level of intimacy in the conversation.

"It was as if we were speaking the same language," Jonathan said to me.

As the conversation continued, Jonathan later asked what the young man thought about the United States being in his home country. The young man's response would make irreversible waves in Jonathan's mind even years after he returned back home to the states.

"It's great but as soon as you all leave, we're going to go back to how we were," the young man said to Jonathan.

"Thank you for the clean water and the food," he interjected.

"But this is Afghanistan,"

"We've lived like this for centuries, it's our way of living."

"It really just felt like it was the two of us," Jonathan said to me.

"Nothing else mattered."

After their conversation, Jonathan proceeded to make the hard ask and follow orders by asking the young man if he'd consider attending the community meeting.

"I remember thinking this guy is so young and has so much potential to be a leader in his community."

To Jonathan's surprise, the young man said yes.

And this brought Jonathan an unbelievable amount of gratification. He knew that this could mean so much more than they could have ever imagined.

Traditionally, at the community meetings, the young people from the village were never really encouraged to speak up or share their ideas for the future of their community. Elders were the ones that were given the authority over the entire conversation and there was little to no intent to include younger leaders.

This, as Jonathan saw it then and sees it today, were fundamental barriers to democracy.

With a radiant smile on his face, Jonathan slowly stood up and gestured that both men "shake on it."

"You're going to the meeting, right?" he reminded the young man one last time.

"Yes." the young responded with certainty.

"You sure?" Jonathan continued.

"Yeah." the young man responded smiling coyly.

Once the interaction was over, Jonathan couldn't help but feel moved by the amount of candor that this man had shared with him.

His response would forever stay in Jonathan's mind. It was, in fact, the catalyst that ignited Jonathan's questioning of the mission of the US Army, his purpose, and ultimately his life's work.

Why were troops on the ground?

Why were they pushing a westernized mindset of democratization on to the people of Afghanistan?

What for—if as soon as the troops left things were going to go right back to how things were before?

Jonathan tied these thoughts and his experience of growing up Latinx in the United States so eloquently:

"Similar to growing up Latinx in America, you're seen as 'the other'. You're constantly being called a minority."

"It's almost as if being Latinx in the US inherently requires *us* to change. As if it requires us to do the changing and assimilating *in order to* thrive in this country."

"We constantly wanted the Afghan people and the Afghan government to be more like us—but what for?" he continued to share passionately.

He described the people he met, the experiences that they shared with him, and how Afghan people genuinely lived their lives as happy.

"They were not sad like you would expect them to be."

"They were the happiest people," he said to me with warmth.

Jonathan had no argument to go against what the young man had shared with him because everything that the young man said was true.

If you must know, Jonathan had no idea whether the young man would in fact follow through on his promise of attending the meeting.

Weeks later, he asked the same interpreter who had facilitated their interaction if he had shown up, and he said yes.

This was everything.

This would be the start of a transformative journey for Jonathan both personally and professionally as a remarkable grassroots community organizer. As he continues to serve this country, in a wildly different yet still similar capacity now, he sees this part of his journey and story as the ultimate ignition of his commitment to organizing and building power to acknowledge the roots and identity of those who have been, more often than not, seen as powerless.

CHAPTER 7

KEVIN SAUCEDO-BROACH

———

In 2017, in a small, quaint, and rather unassuming neighborhood in the state of Virginia, Kevin Saucedo-Broach met an individual that would make an indelible mark on his purpose and ultimately, his passion.

The first image I ever saw of Kevin online was the kind of image that brings you a subtle rush of joy when you see it—no matter how many times you encounter it afterward. Kevin was wearing what looks like a navy button down, a bright-blue bandana around his forehead, and a scrunched-up Pride flag around his neck. Although you can't clearly confirm that it's a Pride flag, for those of us who have had the privilege of attending a Pride parade, you know that smile well.

It's the kind of smile that you can recognize from a million yards away. What was so captivating about this image in particular was how even as Kevin stood in front of a handful of unrecognizable faces in the background, his smile was disarming. It's the kind that draws you in unabashedly and reminds you of the undeniable power that is held in it.

So, on March 30, 2020—smack dab in the middle of a global pandemic—Kevin and I hopped on the phone for the first time to talk about his journey in community engagement, politics, and beyond.

Kevin is the proud son of a Peruvian father and an American mother and calls the state of Virginia home. He currently serves as the chief of staff to the House Democratic Whip Alfonso Lopez in the Virginia House of Delegates.

In 2017, Kevin found himself in the thick of a Democratic coordinated campaign in Virginia. After the election of the 45th president, Kevin knew that this was the right time for him to get on board to something that he profoundly believed in.

After working for the Mayor of the District of Columbia Muriel Bowser, he made the decision to accept the offer to join the team of then-gubernatorial candidate Ralph Northam as an organizer in South Arlington, Virginia. Now-governor Ralph Northam campaigned on one of the most liberal platforms in the commonwealth's modern history. He advocated for a $15 minimum wage, the issue of driver's licenses for undocumented immigrants, in-state tuition for these same students, free community college or apprenticeships for Virginians, early-childhood education, ban on all corporate political giving, and gun control.[8]

---

8   Fenit Nirappil, "What Virginia's Governor-elect Ralph Northam (D) promised during his campaign," *Washington Post*, November 23, 2017.

The stakes for this election for Democrats nationally were considered, by many, to be very high. The Democratic party had failed to win any significant races since the 2016 election.[9]

There was no question about it: the race had so much at stake not just for Democrats in the State of Virginia, but for both sides of the aisle. Outside Northern Virginia, Republicans dominated swaths of the state particularly where the population and the economy were flat or declining.

Kevin still vividly remembers his first training on the job. It was a training that brought a crude reality to the surface. The leaders for the Democratic coordinated campaign gathered all two hundred organizers in one large conference room. As Kevin looked around to his right and left, in the brightly lit room, he quickly noticed that he was one of maybe only five Latinxs in the room. This realization was nothing less than striking.

We all know the feeling; the kind that is both propelling and daunting. Enraging yet hopeful. Enraging because you know they are tokenizing you and it's clear that they don't see or understand or have the ability to grasp the power of representation.

Hopeful because although you'd wish there were more of us in these rooms, *you're* at least there. You're hopeful in the most glorious of ways because you know you're there—in that specific room, in this precise moment in the universe—*for a reason.*

---

9   Michael Tackett, "In Virginia Governor's Race, Immigrants' Turnout May Be Key, " *New York Times*, October 28, 2017.

And Kevin would soon realize just how much this rang true when during one serene fall afternoon the campaign sent him to a neighborhood in Fredericksburg, Virginia. This was right before the end of the Get Out the Vote campaign, the weekend before the election and the team had selected their best performing organizers to run across the finish line of their voter engagement efforts in the area. Fredericksburg, specifically, was deemed a priority as it historically faced low turnout rates due to the insufficient Spanish-speaking political infrastructure.

Wearing slacks and a warm jacket to bear the drizzling rain, Kevin knocked on a door of a modest single-family home. There was nothing quite unordinary about the house per se. Nothing that seemed memorable which would end being a complete contrast to what was actually waiting for Kevin just behind the front door.

Two delicate knocks and a patient wait was all it took for someone to open the door. The woman that opened the door stood at about five feet tall, rather small in comparison to Kevin who stood at 6-foot-1. She was a mature woman, quite older, if you will. She sported beautiful white hair and round, unobtrusive glasses.

"I'm a volunteer and I'm here to talk to you about the upcoming election," Kevin said.

She shook her head and ran back into her house. To Kevin's good fortune, she left the door open.

She wasn't rejecting his presence which, to him, was a hopeful sign that she'd be open to listening or having a conversation at the very least. The woman then came back to the doorway with another woman by her side. This woman, you could hardly ever forget.

Kevin describes her as the quintessential Latinx abuelita. She had a smooth and dark complexion and wore a white-laced Catholic head covering with a long imposing skirt.

"This is someone who is clearly devout," Kevin thought to himself. He, for one, couldn't say the same, as he wasn't particularly religious at all.

He kindly introduced himself to her the same way he had done to the first woman who had welcomed him.

"Mi hijito, de donde eres?" she asked.

"I'm from Virginia pero mi papá es de Perú," Kevin answered.

Upon hearing those words come out of Kevin's mouth, this woman lit up. Her face and her entire being radiated with unexpected joy. But not for the reason that you think, as she was Bolivian after all.

"I cannot believe there is another South American walking around here talking about politics," she exclaimed.

"Y a que iglesia vas," she asked politely.

"No voy a la iglesia," Kevin explained with an ounce of hesitancy and worry that she would be put off by the truth, his truth.

To the surprise of many, it didn't change a thing in their interaction or their connection. And this was the beginning of a long and touching conversation where they spoke about the importance of this election for the people of the commonwealth of Virginia. They spoke about how the election could impact hundreds of people, just like her and Kevin.

And most of all, they spoke about fear. The fear that she had to face knowing that this country had a racist, xenophobic bigot in the highest office in the land.

"I'm terrified," she confessed. Kevin shared that sentiment with her, and right as the conversation began to come to an end, this woman proceeded to run back into the house.

Leaving Kevin, once again, in an absolute limbo of uncertainty in the doorway. He didn't mind though, and he patiently waited for her to come back.

What or whom could she be bringing, he thought.

To Kevin's surprise, she brought back a small travel-sized picture of the Virgin Mary. She looked up at him and with her eyes fiercely yet warmly focused on his, she pressed the picture of la Virgen María into the palms of his hands.

"La Virgen María te va a proteger por que estás haciendo la obra de Dios," she said as she firmly grabbed Kevin by the shoulders.

"Cuidate mucho, mijo. Buena suerte."

This moment made a mark in Kevin's life that he'd never forget. Never before had he been quite literally blessed canvassing and never before had he felt such a personal connection to a complete stranger who certainly didn't feel like one after all.

Kevin went about his way to the rest of the neighborhood and never saw that woman again. Ralph Northam ended up winning the governorship, but this moment stayed forever in Kevin's heart and mind.

What's more is that it's a fervent reminder, to him, of why he does what he does. To him, it's quite simple: Imagine how many people would not have voted in this election if they did not have someone come speak to them in their own language. People, like this woman, and so many of our tías and abuelitas have been purposefully kept out. This system wasn't built for them, that's no secret, but it's the resiliency of those who keep showing up and representing these communities despite these realities that truly hold the power to change this country for the better.

CHAPTER 8

DIOMARA DELVALLE

"That's how *dark* they look," said the light-skinned Puerto Rican girl as she pointed to a dark-skinned classmate on the other side of the cafeteria. She said it with a hint of disgust and a subtle sense of poignancy.

"That's how *Panamanians* look," she continued.

"Dark, dark like *that*." she uttered as she continued to point her finger boldly in the air without a care in the world.

DioMara lifted her eyes from her lunch up towards the girl who was speaking. She didn't know this girl. She wasn't friends with her. She had just been assigned to the same table as her that day for lunch.

DioMara hoped that she misheard. She hoped that at the other end of that finger there wasn't the other dark boy in her school. There were just a few Black kids in that school and DioMara— unknowingly—was one of them. She wished that she had just mistakenly misheard and wouldn't have to face this moment. She held on tight to that specific wish, but a part of her knew that on the other side of that finger there would be someone and something that she could never unsee.

When DioMara brought herself to look at the boy that this young light-skinned Latina was pointing at, her world came to a halt. The boy stood there, harmless. He was speaking to three boys that were near him. He wasn't doing *anything to anyone*. Yet, the color of his skin was his greatest weakness.

DioMara couldn't believe the words that had come out of this girl's mouth. She looked back at the girl making these remarks and she looked down again at herself—at her own arms. Slowly, she felt her world shatter in that moment. Her chest felt heavy. Her body started to feel like it was shrinking into the bench as she slowly processed what had been said.

"I don't look like that," she remembers thinking to herself.

"Do I look like that?" she continued to question.

Moments of silence and deep despair transpired before DioMara came to a stark realization, a realization that would take her nearly a decade to make peace with.

She, too, was "dark like that".

She, too, was Panamanian.

She looked up to see the boy's skin tone one more time just to be faced with the same gruesome reality.

At 13, she was already dealing with anxiety and, like so many at that age, she was afraid of speaking up. She was afraid of speaking out. Still unable to fully process what had just happened, she stayed in silence.

DioMara's mind started to race in a million different directions.

"Am I not supposed to look this way?" she thought to herself.

She asked, "Was I created incorrectly?"

"Maybe we ended up in the wrong place," she contemplated as she thought about her family and her heritage.

"Maybe something wrong happened that made my family look this way?" she continued.

Again, she felt the urge to respond. Was it really responding? It wasn't said to her exactly, but it felt like it was directly aimed at her and to her. Yet, the urge persisted. She wanted to say something to that girl right then and there, but she couldn't find the right words. She couldn't find the right thing to say or the tone to say it in.

What would she say, after all? How would others react? How would this make her look in front of her peers? What consequences could come from this?

She looked around one last time to, ultimately, find the room completely unbothered. A disconnect between her world and the rest. A disconnect that she would later find perpetuated

in her own Latinx community. A blatant disregard— at best—
of people whose hue didn't match hers—people who spoke
the same tongue that was spoken at home yet failed to see her
as one of their own. At worst, the perpetuation of otherness,
an exclusion from the feeling of belonging.

DioMara, at the tender age of thirteen, had just begun the
rollercoaster of her teenage years. For her and for so many
others, those years were replete with anxiety, shyness, and to
some extent, the difficult journey of having to wrestle with
her own identity as a Black Panamanian American girl and
soon-to-be woman.

However, the story doesn't quite end there. It gets better
and better.

Just a couple years later, at fifteen years old, that shy little
girl would find herself performing at the world-famous
Apollo Theater. The theater where legends like the Jackson
Five, Diana Ross, Whitney Houston, Billie Holiday, Stevie
Wonder, Luther Vandross, Aretha Franklin, Marvin Gaye,
and many others have graced the stage.

"If I can get past the Harlem audience...then—for me—that's
an indication that I'm ready to move on," DioMara remembers thinking before getting on stage.

The audience at the Apollo Theater has, historically, been
hard to please. Nevertheless, performing with everything
that she could possibly give of herself, DioMara won the
crowd over. She even went on to perform at the Apollo Theater two more times after that.

As a proud Panamanian American, this would be the beginning of an incredible journey in DioMara's artistry, talent, and power—a journey that never ends.

CHAPTER 9

KEVIN LIMA

———

I'll always remember the look on the face of my property manager at my apartment building in Washington, DC as I ran across the lobby carrying three different dresses in garment bags over my shoulder while also wearing heels and a dress.

"Are you still having events?" he asked with a concerned expression on his face and a genuine aura of alarm.

I remember laughing slightly uncomfortably but also genuinely feeling amused as I realized just how this scene might be perceived by him and others.

It wasn't the first time that the staff saw me walking out of the building in very unexpected formal attire but it certainly *would* be my last.

It was March 19, 2020.

The World Health Organization, just a few days prior, had declared the rapidly spreading COVID-19 outbreak a global pandemic and people were just starting to catch on to the severity of the situation at hand. I think in some way or another, we all have that specific day in mid or early March 2020 where we can vividly recall everything changing. March 19 was that day for me.

"I've got to do this thing for the book I'm writing and then I'm leaving to go to my parents' home in the suburbs," I responded.

I was the Associate Director for Workplace Equality at the Human Rights Campaign at the time, and all staff had been notified of the new work-from-home measures that were going to be implemented.

I had about two hours to pack up for what I thought would be a three-week, four-week stay—at the most—at my parents' home, get ready, and take promotional pictures for the official announcement for the book all before hopping on the phone with Kevin.

I remember sending Kevin a quick note that same morning asking if we could push back our call just to be safe and make sure that I had enough time and was in the right headspace to speak with him.

I also remember being so intrigued when I first came across Kevin and his work as the Youth Political Director at the Democratic National Committee. He had an extensive record mobilizing and engaging youth all across the country so I knew that he would, unequivocally, be someone I wanted to interview for this book.

I reached out to him a few weeks before our scheduled call and he came off in the best way possible. His light really shined through even when our interactions were limited to just text and emails.

After running around the city trying to take what I hoped would be the perfect pictures to officially announce the book, I sat down in my partially immaculate, partially imperceptibly messy DC apartment to get ready for our call.

I felt energized with a hint of excitement and an ounce of terror for the unknown—for what might come from this pandemic.

I remember taking a moment to quietly think about how this global pandemic might affect the trajectory of this book. Would people still be open to letting me interview them for this book? Would it be insensitive or inconsiderate to write this during a time where people's mind and bodies were consumed with how they might make rent next month or if they had a chance to lose a loved one?

I hopped on the phone with Kevin and completely escaped from any doubt I had about my *why* for this book.

It was that call with Kevin, for me. It was his willingness to be vulnerable, honest, and unimaginably generous with his story to a complete stranger that he had never met before. His story moved me to my core.

On May 7, 2016, more than thirteen thousand students walked across the stage to graduate from Pennsylvania State

University. One of them was Kevin Lima. As he walked on to the stage and followed the procession of thousands of students who, like him, looked out into the sea of people in hopes of finding a familiar face, a smile they recognize, a cheer or yell from someone they love, he had the distinct memory of a time when things were much simpler, yet much more complex. Perhaps a combination of the two.

He remembered himself—a six-year-old boy in the early 2000s on a hot summer day in Los Angeles, California. He was across the country and thousands of miles away from where he was now, standing in an empty house. Empty not because it was his own or his families, empty because it wasn't.

From ages five to twelve, Kevin's parents took him to work with them because they couldn't afford to pay for childcare. For those of us who can relate to this experience, you know that these circumstances—in the end—were blessings in disguise, and this rings true for Kevin as well.

He remembers spending his summers in homes that weren't his but felt familiar. His mother cleaned the house, his father painted them, and his tío fixed the electricity. It was a team effort of course and even the kids, Kevin and his cousin, took part.

"Pónganse a trabajar y si ustedes hacen un buen trabajo, les compramos McDonalds," he remembers his mother saying. Although Kevin felt responsible enough to handle the vacuum, Kevin's mother only trusted him with the squeegee.

A six-year-old's hand and a squeegee. It was those same hands that were now holding a college diploma—*his* college diploma. It was this same person who was now wearing a cap and a gown. A proud son of a woman who cleaned houses and a father who painted them.

It was this child, now a full-fledged adult, who was told he was a minority, time and time again while he was growing up, but when he looked around at his classmates and his classrooms, he certainly didn't feel like one.

Kevin knew that the stage he was crossing now was certainly not made for him or people who looked like him. Yet, there he was. Nevertheless, he persisted. His crossing of that stage would ignite a remarkable journey in political engagement of one of the most powerful, most diverse electorates in this country—the youth.

Kevin went on to get the first Latina ever elected to the US Senate, Senator Catherine Cortez Masto, and has devoted his career to mobilize hundreds of thousands of young voters under the age of thirty-five to vote. *He* did that all before thirty. And this is just the beginning.

CHAPTER 10

MARIZOL LEYVA

"We are finally creating a unity in the community that was never there before," Marizol Leyva said to me with an overwhelming amount of conviction. It was the kind that permeates any barrier of restrained vulnerability that you ever felt hesitant to share.

Marizol Leyva is, without a doubt, one of the most passionate people I've had the pleasure of interviewing for this book. Her radiance and determination for the resilient activism and representation of the Afro-Latinx transgender community is absolutely incomparable.

As soon as I heard about *My Sister: How One Sibling's Transition Changed Us Both*, a joint memoir written by Marizol and her sister, *Orange Is the New Black* star Selenis Leyva, I knew right then and there that I wanted to do everything in my power to be able to interview Marizol for this book.

I remember the distinct hesitation I felt at first. Marizol is remarkably impressive. She is a nationally recognized activist, a transgender model, cook, podcast host, and most recently, a published author who has been featured in magazines like *Vogue México*, *Time*, *Cosmopolitan*, and *Latina*, just to name a few.

It was certainly a long shot, but I was pleasantly surprised and thrilled to get an unequivocal "of course" from Marizol almost immediately after reaching out to her on Instagram. She was a light even from thousands of miles away.

Marizol grew up in a proud Cuban family in the Bronx where perceptions of gender and sexuality were tremendously restrictive. Marizol, from a young age, knew that she was a girl and felt that she was born in the wrong body.

"I have *always* been Marizol," she said to me with a smile that was perceivable even through the phone.

As early as she can possibly remember, Marizol was drawn to stereotypically "girly" things, as she would happily play with her sister's clothes, put a t-shirt over her head and pretend it was long hair—actions that were most certainly frowned upon in her household, especially by her father.

Difficulties began to intensify for Marizol when she entered high school. Even as she outwardly presented as male and dressed in a stereotypically "masculine" way, the bullying didn't subside as she would get harassed for "talking" and "walking" like a girl.

"Those times were really difficult," she shared with me.

Although Marizol faced and overcame a remarkable amount of challenges both internally and externally, she remembers a distinct time when she felt as though she was finally stepping into her power, reclaiming her identity, and unveiling her purpose in this world.

On October 11, 2017, when Marizol was twenty-four years old, her sister, Selenis, asked her to accompany her to the annual Anti-Violence Project Courage Awards in New York City.

The Anti-Violence Project, AVP, was formed in 1980 as a response to a series of brutal attacks against the LGBTQ+ community in the streets of Chelsea. From its early start organizing, engaging community members, and taking to the streets, the organization has expanded to provide free, confidential counseling to LGBTQ+ survivors of all forms of violence including hate violence, intimate partner violence, sexual violence, police violence, and HIV-related violence.

Selenis had been asked to present an award to her *Orange is the New Black* co-star, Laverne Cox. Laverne is an Emmy-nominated actress, documentary film producer, as well as a leading national transgender rights activist and powerhouse. In 2014, she became the first openly transgender person to appear on the cover of *Time Magazine*. Her representation on screen as well as off has, undoubtedly, transformed and advanced the entertainment industry far beyond somewhere anybody else has ever taken it. Not only did she win a Primetime Emmy Award in the acting category for her role in *Orange Is the New Black*, but she was also the first transgender woman to win a Daytime Emmy as an executive producer for her own documentary, *Laverne Cox Presents: The T Word*. However, her influence goes beyond just the reach of masses. Her influence also made a difference in how Selenis Leyva viewed her own sister, Marizol.

In an article in *People* magazine, Selenis explained:

"When I met Laverne, I remember thinking, 'I'm going to watch her.'

"I thought, 'How is this going to play out? Is this character going to be a respectful representation or is it going to be fluff and surface?'

"Laverne and I had our conversations, I told her I had a transgender sister. But I was so thrilled, not only that the character had so many layers and was beautifully written, but also because of Laverne's ability to convey her thoughts and feelings in a way that made you listen that I knew would be really impactful."[10]

Laverne's influence on Selenis' understanding of her own sister had transcended anything that Selenis ever expected. So, that night at the awards ceremony, as she saw both Laverne and Selenis together sitting at a table as she gave her speech on the stage, she declared to every single person in that room that she had a transgender sister.

Marizol remembers the rush of energy that she felt in her body as she looked into the distance and saw her sister say

---

10   Morgan Smith, "OITNB's Selenis Leyva: Working with Laverne Cox Helped Me Understand My Trans Sister's Journey," *People Magazine*, March 24, 2020.

those words in public for the first time. For years, Marizol had been hiding her identity as a transgender woman and this would the very first time that she declared it to the world.

Marizol had just ended an abusive relationship with a man who made her feel ashamed of who she was as a transgender woman, and she finally had been starting to feel as though she was beginning to reclaim herself, her identity, her dignity, and her self-worth. She had never before disclosed her identity as a transgender woman, so this moment was monumental.

"It was magical." she said to me.

After years of constantly hiding and suppressing that side of herself, Marizol was finally free—embracing herself and her experiences wholeheartedly. And what's more is that she was doing it with the support of other Black transgender women, like Laverne and so many others. She was doing it in community, and she was not alone.

Now, after releasing *My Sister: How One Sibling's Transition Changed Us Both*, she has found her voice and her purpose in fiercely advocating for the rights of Black transgender women like herself. Her mere unapologetic existence continues to make waves and change the landscape for Afro-Latinx queer, non-binary, and transgender people all over this nation.

CHAPTER 11

DASH HARRIS

—

On a warm and mellow Tuesday afternoon, Dash Harris and I hopped on a phone call with a sea between us—Dash in Panamá and myself on the East Coast. A call that was initially supposed to be 30-45 minutes evolved into a two-and-a-half-hour conversation that effectively changed the trajectory of how I viewed anti-Blackness and white supremacy within the Latinx community.

Dash Harris is, without question, a force like no other. She is a founder, a thought leader, a multimedia journalist, and a documentarian who has been featured on CNN, *USA Today*, The Root, *Latina* magazine, HipLatina, and the Huffington Post—just to name a few.

However, beyond the accolades and the well-deserved recognition, there exists a deeply transformative side to Dash's work as well.

In 2010, after Dash's graduation from Temple University with a degree in journalism, she quickly embarked on a mission to get a coveted role in her field and moved to New York

City. In the midst of securing an apartment, she was determined to do whatever it took to secure a job at CNN. She had previously visited the Time Warner building and met several members of the team at CNN, so she knew that it was up to her whether she leveraged those interactions in order to obtain a full-time job opportunity. She knew that she had to find a way to get in contact with the right person who would be able to help her get her foot in the door. And so, the venture began.

As she looked at the business cards she had previously been able to acquire during her last visit, she noticed that the only difference between all of the phone numbers that were listed on the business cards were the last four digits. With the encouragement and pep talk from Dash's dear friend, Renita, she gathered up the courage to pick up the phone and make the call. No, not an infamous "hope you are well" email, but a bold phone call where she would face the reality head on.

Knowing that the morning show aired at 9 a.m., she knew that folks on the team would be on-site anywhere from 1 a.m. to 3 a.m. With that in mind, Dash stayed up all night to make sure she dialed the show's executive assistant promptly before 3 a.m.

Without personally knowing whom she was calling, Dash dialed the phone number and did so unapologetically.

"You don't know me but I applied for this job," she remembers blurting out fearlessly to the person at the other end of the line.

Not knowing if this would be a complete fail or not, she was pleasantly surprised by the response she received.

"I'll make sure you get an interview," the person replied.

Days later, she was back at the Time Warner building feeling as energized as ever. Her bold, fearless move proved to work and there was no stopping her at this point. She showed up to that interview with the lead producers without a single thought of holding back. Dash's mother, a proud Panamanian, always stressed the importance of preparation—of knowing your stuff in order to get ahead. She instilled in her daughter the belief that no one was going to make anything happen for her and it was up to Dash to give the very best of herself and fight for what she wanted.

Naturally, being her mother's daughter, Dash researched every single detail of the person she was to have this interview with. She knew all of the information that she could possibly know about them.

So, that day, as she walked into the front of the Time Warner building, Dash walked into her power with every single ounce of conviction in the world—staying true to the roots that had been instilled in her.

It certainly served her well. The lead producers gave her a significant amount of positive praise for her boldness that day and a few weeks later, after another round of interviews, she got the job.

One detail that is very revealing of just what kind of person Dash is that Dash made the leap to move to New York City from Philadelphia *before* she secured her job at CNN. It was detail I remember flinching at when I first heard, but after we finished our conversation that afternoon, I was not surprised by in the slightest.

"I moved December 31, 2008," she said to me.

On that day, Dash moved into an incandescent three-bedroom apartment in Harlem with the help of her dear friend Tara. At this point, she was impatiently awaiting a response to move on to the final round of interviews at CNN.

"Look, I don't have any money," she said to her soon-to-be landlord when they first met.

She knew that it was long shot, but Dash took it anyway. A move that so many of us could not even fathom pulling off.

Due to President Obama's inauguration as the 44th President of the United States, her next interview at CNN had been significantly delayed. Dash needed to find a way to sustain herself in the meantime. Her cousin, who did taxes as one of her streams of income, offered her a job and Dash assisted her in servicing her clients during that year's tax season to be able to put a roof over her head for that period of time.

Several weeks later, on the week of February 9, 2009, Dash was once again called in for her final interview. This time, Dash was set to be interviewed by then Vice President of Programming for CNN Janelle Rodriguez. Janelle, a fellow Afro-Latina, led all daytime and weekend programming for the network. When Dash arrived for what was expected to be the final round of interviews, Janelle not only praised Dash for her bold initiative to call, but she also told her to go down to Human Resources immediately and complete her paperwork.

Dash, stunned at the brevity of the interview, couldn't help but to think of all the incredible Black women who had supported her through this. From her mother's unyielding encouragement, her friend Renita's pep talk as she began to scope out her outreach strategy, to her cousin who helped her make some money while the job came through, to Janelle Rodriguez who believed in Dash's talent and took a chance— it was all coming together.

Over the next year, Dash worked as a production assistant at CNN. During this time, she realized that she was not feeling fulfilled or even happy with the work that she was doing.

"This isn't why I wanted to be in news," she remembers thinking to herself.

She was a witness to not only how white supremacy thrived in the industry but also a witness to the unnerving loyalty that came with it. The way she was treated, as a Black female, was radically different than how her white counterparts were treated.

"It was like night and day," she recalls.

There was one particular instance that she recalls vividly. His name was Spencer, no less. And he was also a production assistant just like Dash. One morning he called out of work to candidly share with his supervisor that he was "too drunk and too hungover" to come into work that day.

"You would never say that," Dash remembers thinking to herself. However, he knew that his white executive producer would give him the required protection to allow this behavior to happen and allow that same behavior to continue.

Unfortunately, these moments went far beyond that. The invisibility and disregard were quite prevalent in Dash's workplace with the team at CNN. For example, Dash would go into the break room for a coffee or to warm her lunch and, naturally, she would give a cordial "good morning" or "good afternoon" to the person who was sharing the same space. However, her cordial greeting was met with indifference, disregard, and a normalized lack of acknowledgement. They would look her dead in the eye and keep it moving. Not with any malicious intent, but just a dumbfounding and crude reality of how toxic the culture was.

For anyone who had been raised to give others common courtesy, it was a hard realization to swallow. During these times, Dash's mother was her guiding light.

"Don't let strangers change you," she would say to Dash.

"They shouldn't have the power to change you. They are the ones that have to look at themselves in the mirror at the end of the day, and they are the ones that have to cry themselves to sleep."

"Nothing that is happening outside of yourself matters" she would say to Dash poignantly.

In the midst of being in that type of environment, it was imperative for Dash to rely on her community. Her community was composed of strong Black women. One of the women that she met at work one day said, "Listen—when you're done with your shift—come to my desk."

There, she broke down the politics of the office with Dash.

"Be cordial to everyone," she said.

"But know that you need to do what you came here to do."

She shared this information with Dash because she knew, firsthand, how much sabotaging existed in the office. It was sabotaging that was taking place among *white women* in the office.

She witnessed it and saw the damage that came from it and she did not want Dash being caught in the middle of it. It was the generosity of these Black women who wanted the best for Dash that allowed her to rise above through this period in her life. And while she was tremendously grateful for their support and encouragement throughout this chapter in her life, Dash could feel that she wanted something more out of her professional career—both on a personal and professional level.

"This is not what I set out to do," Dash remembers thinking to herself.

Because she worked for a morning production, her schedule would consist of getting into the office at 2 a.m., 4 a.m., or even 5 a.m. and leaving at 9 a.m, a schedule that for most would seem nearly impossible. This schedule, though, also allowed her to visit her family in Pennsylvania as often as she wanted. Dash would hop on a two-hour bus to visit her family in Buschill. A couple hours after that, she arrived at her family's home and shared her change of plans. She told her mom she wanted to quit her job at CNN and embark on a journey to explore identity, colonization, racism, and the African Diaspora in Latin America. Dash's mother had always been a supporter of big, audacious dreams.

"Quit. Quit. Quit," her mother cheered.

"She would always support any idea of mine no matter how unconventional or different it might have seemed to others," Dash recalls.

This is when Dash embarked on a remarkable journey to produce NEGRO: a docu-series that explores the effects of colonization, colorism, racism, stereotypes, and media representation of Black Latin Americans.

This unparalleled venture was born out of Dash's innate interest in learning more about the resilience of the descendants of the African Diaspora in Latin America and the Caribbean. Through candid interviews with Black Latin Americans in Colombia, Perú, the Dominican Republic, Brazil, and Puerto Rico, Dash was able to start to unveil how these people viewed themselves and how society viewed them within the confines of race and color.

Encouraged by a gross miseducation and misperception of what being Latinx in the United States was largely understood to be, Dash set out to deconstruct the social manifestations and consequences of the deep-rooted color and class complex. The docu-series goes on to explore the history behind how these perceptions were formed and shines light on the attitudes of race, color, self-identification, and how it all informs the social interactions among Black and non-Black Latin Americans.

It's no surprise that for those of us who have had the privilege to not have to think about the color of our skin and how it stains the lens in which we are viewed as people—whether that be in Latin America or here in the United States—these conversations can be abrasive or startling at first. However, that's no excuse when it comes to confronting your own responsibility to face and, in your own capacity, to begin to unlearn the deep-rooted anti-Blackness that we've all, in one way or another, taken part in or benefitted from.

In her latest Refinery29 article entitled "No, I'm Not A Proud Latina," Dash writes:

I am here because of my Negritud, my Blackness, and in spite of Latinidad. Latinidad, Hispanidad, "La Raza Cosmica" (The Cosmic Race), "La Raza" (the race)—are all manifestations of hegemonic, white European domination and subjugation—and it continues to be. Ironically, for all the theatrics of this "cosmic Latin" race, Latinx—merely, a geographical identifier—has never been a race nor an ethnicity. How could over twenty countries share a singular ethnicity?

I am a Black Panamanian with Antillean and colonial Panamanian roots. Afro-Panamanians may be descendants of

Africans, free and enslaved, during the colonial period as well as descendants of Afro-Caribbeans from Anglo and Francophone Caribbean countries whose labor built major agriculture and infrastructure projects of the country. While the nation was built by Africans and Afro descendants trafficked to Panama and migrated for labor, dominant white culture simultaneously rejected and exploited our existence.

My "ethnicity" and "Latin" commonalities with a rabiblanco (white Panamanian) or an indigenous Panamanian starts and ends at citizenship. A citizenship that Panama's eugenicist, US-educated, Hitler-idolizing thrice-president Arnulfo Arias revoked from Black Caribbean Panamanians, who he referred to as "parasitic races". In 1941, he recommended sterilization to stop the degeneration of the country and "improve the race." This is language that many people in Panama still use to describe specific classes of Black people to this day. What "race" exactly did Arias mean to "improve"? Not mine and not the millions who look like me. I am exploited and buried for Latinidad to flourish. My body trampled to mantle New Spain's blood-soaked banner knitted with the bones of my ancestors.[11]

This is what I find most transformative about Dash's work. She didn't stop after NEGRO. That was only the tip of the iceberg in her journey. She, along with her fellow co-founders of Radio Caña Negra, Evelyn Alvarez, and Janvieve Williams, unapologetically call out the dehumanization of Black Latinxs both in the United States and Latin America and talk

---

11   "No, I'm Not A Proud Latina," Refinery29, accessed October 1, 2020.

about the ways in which non-Black Latinxs have failed and continue to fail Black people.

Through webinars and educational seminars, they not only continue to defiantly stand up against the anti-Blackness within our community, but they pave a new standard for what the fight against white supremacy should and needs to look like in the United States and beyond.

PART 3

ACTION

CHAPTER 12

ANTONIO ARELLANO

———

In February of 1994, Antonio Arellano woke up and found himself in a booster seat in the back of a car he did not recognize. He distinctly remembers it being cold, dark, and eerily quiet. He was three years old.

In the driver's seat, there was a man whom he did not recognize.

To the right of the driver, was a woman whom he did not recognize either.

"'Cierra los ojos y hazte el dormido," the man in the driver's seat said to Antonio sternly.

The car suddenly started moving forward.

Afraid of what might come next, Antonio did as he was told and shut his eyes. As soon as he did, an indomitable white light penetrated his thin eyelids. Instead of the warmth of pure darkness, of absolute unknown, Antonio had to face an unknown that was startlingly present.

Antonio, who was filled with fear and confusion, like any child might be in that situation, refused to open his eyes even though every single ounce of his body made him want to see where he was and what was happening. The mere desire of wanting to face the reality in front of him was paralyzing.

The car continued to move forward.

"These are my children," the man in the driver's seat said to someone that seemed to be outside of the car.

Antonio listened closely for a response to this statement and heard nothing.

"I was completely oblivious to what was going on," he recalls.

After the white light subsided, he finally felt safe to open his eyes again. As the driver parked the car, in the distance, Antonio saw a face that he *did* recognize.

It was his father—waiting for him with open arms.

He quickly undid the seatbelt that was restraining him and ran towards his dad. He ran as fast as he possibly could.

He ran into the arms of his father and embraced him with every single emotion and ounce of energy that he had in him.

This exact moment proved to be the biggest embrace of his life.

"Mijo you're safe now" Antonio's dad said to him.

Antonio was now on American soil—safe in his father's arms and about to begin an extraordinary journey filled with unimaginable difficulties and unfathomable victories.

There isn't a more perfect embodiment of Latinx Excellence than Antonio Arellano.

After immigrating to the United States that cold winter day in Texas, Antonio and his family moved to the state of Georgia where he grew up in a middle-class neighborhood in the city of Dalton.

Antonio, gay and undocumented, attended Southeast Whitfield High School, a high school that was incredibly conservative. It was a place where the sight of confederate flags wasn't the least bit rare.

In his junior year of high school, Antonio told his father that he wanted to become a journalist. Inspired by Latinx anchors like Maria Elena Salinas and Jorge Ramos, Antonio wanted to be a voice for his own community.

"I remember watching two powerful people that looked like me encapsulate American history, like the tragic September 11, 2001 attacks, and the election of the first Black president in November 2008. I too wanted to help write the first draft of history, like they did."

He shared these desires with his father, and he gave Antonio a response that he wasn't expecting.

Antonio's father told him that, where they were from in Michoacán, Mexico, journalists are either poor or get killed.

The conversation was left there.

A year later, much to Antonio's surprise, his father came to him to resume the conversation.

"I know you want to be a journalist," his father said to him.

"But Dalton doesn't have many media opportunities, what's your plan, mijo?"

Antonio, with the greatest sense of pride, told his father that they needed to pick up and go to Texas.

"Texas. Houston, Texas." he said to him.

"Harris County is home to the largest Latino population in the country. If we want to make an impact on behalf of our growing Latinx community, Texas is ground zero."

Antonio understood the gravity of the situation. He knew that he was making a huge ask.

Months went by and it was now time for Antonio's graduation from high school. He had been selected to give a speech during his commencement ceremony. And knowing that his parents wouldn't be able to understand a single sentence during the ceremony, he fought for his right to be able to say one sentence in Spanish.

At the very end of his speech, Antonio shared the wise words that his father once gave him.

"Mijo, en este mundo puedes tener todo pero tienes que sacrificarte y trabajar duro por el."

"To continue to fight against all odds," he proclaimed in English.

This was the ultimate vindication for him. The ability to even say those words in an auditorium of three hundred people.

He looked at his father and saw tears running down his face. This would be the very first time that Antonio ever saw his father crying.

"Mijo, I'm sorry you can't go to any parties," Antonio's father said to him as they walked to their car after graduation with a demure smile on his face.

This was the moment that changed everything. Antonio's parents had sold everything they owned, his dad quit his job, and they packed what was left in a U-Haul truck.

"You have four years to become a journalist," he said with his eyes about to well up.

The whole family had upended their lives in the state of Georgia and were set to move to Houston, Texas so Antonio could have his shot at becoming a journalist.

Antonio hugged his father with all of the force that he could muster as enthralling memories of that hug when he was three made it back to his mind.

They drove twelve hours that night.

These sacrifices were not in vain. Antonio started building and solidifying his own voice as he continued to be fiercely outspoken about issues around immigration and civil rights. It was because of this voice and this presence that Antonio amassed almost one hundred thousand followers that year and caught the attention of a producer at ABC13 News who immediately was astoundingly impressed at what Antonio had achieved in such a short amount of time.

"You are doing digital better than anybody right now," the producer said to Antonio with a decidedly frank and serious tone.

In 2015, Antonio Arellano was their first ever DACA recipient to get a contract with ABC at their local affiliate as a social media correspondent covering politics and immigration.

One year later, after the 45th president was elected, Antonio had to face one of the most arduous challenges in his professional career up until that point: staying objective amidst the inhumane and hateful rhetoric directed towards not only his own community, but also an overwhelming amount of marginalized communities around the country as well.

In light of this, Antonio continued to denounce these attacks and championed for a forthright unified voice against the dehumanization of immigrant communities.

Just a few years later, in August 2019, Antonio became the interim executive director of Jolt, the largest progressive

Latino organization in Texas, and has been named one of the most influential Latinos in the United States.

Antonio says that being the first openly gay, undocumented executive director of Jolt adds another dimension to the intersectional work that the organization strives to achieve.

"Many of our team members identify as LGBTQ+, and we are predominantly female-led," Arellano said to a reporter at Outsmart Magazine in September of 2019.[12]

Today Antonio uses his voice and platforms to encourage young Latinxs to make systemic change on racial, immigration, economic, environmental, and gender justice issues through leadership development and advocacy.

Antonio is a modern civil rights leader with a thorough understanding of the power of the Latinx vote. He embodies the power of Latinx leadership and the resilience of the immigrant community at its greatest.

In the end, if you ever ask Antonio his *why*, it always comes back to one thing: his family.

---

12   Lourdes Zavaleta, "Man of Action," *OutSmart Magazine*, September 11, 2019, 1.

CHAPTER 13

CARLOS CARDONA

———

"Your choice can choose the next leader of the free world," then-presidential hopeful Barack Obama said to an energetic crowd of supporters in front of the Capitol Building in Concord, New Hampshire.

It was October 22, 2007 and the then-junior senator from the state of Illinois had officially filed his paperwork for the New Hampshire primary.

Wearing an unassuming white button up and black slacks with the sun shining powerfully in the background, he spoke to the dozens of supporters who had gathered to witness him speak.

"So, my question is," he posed.

"Are you fired up?"

"Are you ready to go?"

"Are you fired up," he continued.

"Are you ready to go?"

People cheered and hollered in astonishing support for someone who they thought could lead the state of New Hampshire and be on track to win the Democratic Party's nomination for president.[13]

Although it is hard to even imagine Barack Obama as a political underdog in today's world, things were different back then. Barack Obama's chances for the presidency were starting to look a little shaky at the time. Just two months before the Iowa caucuses and the long-awaited New Hampshire primary, Obama continued to fall further behind Clinton in the national polls.[14] The pressure was on.

A few weeks after this, and ahead of the New Hampshire Democratic primary that was to take place in January of 2008, Carlos Cardona received a phone call to attend the New Hampshire Democratic Party's McIntyre-Shaheen 100 Club dinner. It was an unexpected invitation, no less, but an invitation that was accepted with great pride and gratitude.

Carlos Cardona was seventeen years old at the time. And even then, he was undeniably a force of nature.

Earlier that year, Carlos was pulled over and stopped by a state trooper who asked to see his birth certificate. Realizing

---

13 BarackObamadotcom, "Barack Obama Files for the New Hampshire Primary," October 25, 2007, video, 1:53.

14 Adam Nagourney, "Debate Preview: All Eyes on Obama," *New York Times*, October 30, 2007.

the tragic injustices that this action imposed, Cardona knew that he couldn't stand idly by and take it.

He filed a complaint that reached the Office of the Governor of New Hampshire and, due to this initiative, was later appointed to serve on a gubernatorial taskforce aimed at improving troopers' rapport with local communities of color.

Carlos' journey into politics and social justice, however, started far before that encounter. When Carlos was five, in his native Puerto Rico, his maternal grandfather began carrying him on his shoulder to political rallies on the island.

Carlos, who grew up in an informal settlement in the outskirts of the town of Aguadilla called Campo Alegre on the west coast of Puerto Rico, vividly remembers the activism and political engagement that he witnessed.

By age twelve, Carlos' parents had divorced, and they left Campo Alegre in hopes of a better life in the city of Caguas, which is located at the heart and center of Puerto Rico. There, he moved in with his mother's new partner, who was physically abusive to Carlos' mother. His day-to-day became tougher and tougher as his mother was diagnosed with cancer and had to endure the physical abuse of her partner on top of it all.

"I thought the nightmare would never end," Carlos remembers thinking. However, just when things were the worst he thought they could possibly get, an old friend of his mother's, AnnLee, bought the whole family plane tickets to Haverhill,

Massachusetts. Without much notice, they boarded the plane and left the island.

Diciéndole adiós a una isla amada y comenzando un nuevo capítulo.

Haverhill, Massachusetts, located forty-five minutes north of the city of Boston, seemed like the perfect place to start a new chapter—at least at first. Carlos was fifteen years old then and began exploring and learning more about his sexual orientation. Later that year, when Carlos came out to his mother on Mother's Day, she told him to leave the bedroom they shared.

Without any other options other than to pick up and leave due to the mounting pressure of his mother's cancer diagnosis and Carlos being LGBTQ+, he made the decision to move out. A few months later, Carlos moved in with his partner just outside of Laconia, to the town of Franklin in New Hampshire.

He was seventeen and having to face the challenge of not being able to enroll without parental consent, he ran for the school board and won, making him New Hampshire's youngest elected official.

So, when Carlos received a phone call to attend the New Hampshire Democratic Party's McIntyre-Shaheen 100 Club dinner ahead of the 2008 New Hampshire Democratic primary in January, just a month after winning his election, he accepted the invitation with a great deal of enthusiasm.

The McIntyre-Shaheen 100 Club dinner, a signature event in the state of New Hampshire that is attended by thousands, is usually held to ignite the party base and create an aura of unity within the Democratic Party ahead of the presidential primary.

The dinner, commonly held at the Southern New Hampshire University arena, had seats in the rafters and around eighty tables on the floor with twelve seats each for those who were to attend the sit-down dinner.

Carlos, as naïve as it might sound, wasn't expecting anything out of the ordinary that night. In many ways, he was just beginning his journey as an elected official and the day-to-day life that came with it. However, he had really made a big mistake when he expected that this night would be out of the ordinary because it ended up being a night that Carlos would never forget.

When he arrived at Southern New Hampshire University, and as he made his way around the venue, he saw Michelle Obama standing in the hallway. That year, *Vanity Fair* described her as "regally tall, stunning" and even claimed that she looked "as down to earth as any other soccer mom and as glamorous as a model while instantly commanding respect even before she starts to speak." Even in 2007, as a "First Lady in Waiting," she was as dashing a figure as we consider her today.

So, naturally, Carlos hesitated to go over to her at first but knew that he would regret it if he didn't speak to her when he had the opportunity to do so.

To this extent, after mustering all the courage he could possibly muster at that moment, he went on to approach her. As Carlos began to introduce himself, she kindly said "I heard your story—can you sit at our table?"

He, without a moment's hesitation, accepted the invitation and proceeded to sit next to Michelle Obama.

Let that sink in.

Michelle Obama.

Mrs. Obama, Carlos remembers, was handing out Obama-themed stickers that consisted of the classic 2008 Obama logo but instead of bright green grass, the logo now had a rainbow-patterned soil to show support for the LGBTQ+ electorate.

Once they got to their table, she proceeded to confidently place the sticker on Carlos' chest and after several minutes of conversation asked, "So, are you supporting Barack?"

"I've been thinking about it and it's been tough," he coyly responded.

He kept the answer there. Less was more in this instance because at the time, Hillary Clinton was deemed as *the* candidate that the LGBTQ+ community would stand behind.

As Carlos remembers it, it was Hillary Clinton that was seen as the pioneer for the queer community as LGBTQ+ folks were pushed to the margins in the Republican-dominated Bush era of politics.

Little did we know that *President* Obama just a few years later would flip the conversation on LGBTQ+ rights in just eight years—from the Hate Crimes Prevention Act the first year he was in office, to overturning "Don't Ask Don't Tell", to LGBTQ+ people in leading roles in the Obama White House, to the historical 2011 speech to the United Nations, delivered by then Secretary of State Hillary Clinton, no less.

Nevertheless, they left the topic there. And throughout the night, they spoke about their respective paths and experiences with poverty.

Carlos distinctly remembers how they spoke of poverty in a way that felt real, that felt personal, that felt authentic to those—like himself —who had lived it firsthand. In his mind, at that moment, he thought to himself, "This is it. I've got to support him."

Once they had all sat down at the table for dinner, Barack Obama looked down at the rainbow sticker that his wife had put on Carlos earlier in the night.

"Never forget that you are young, you're LGBT, and you're Latino...that's powerful," he said to Carlos.

Those words would stay with Carlos forever.

Before the night ended, Carlos knew that he had to get something off his chest. With both of them right beside him, he knew that he needed to say what he was feeling before the time spent with them was over.

"The conversations that we have had tonight—they've impacted me more than you can imagine," he said to Michelle.

"I think that it's really important to support Barack because he not only represents young people, but he also represents the struggle of facing poverty," he added.

Carlos would later become the co-chair of the New Hampshire-based LGBTQ+ coalition backing Barack Obama's presidency and the chair of the Laconia Democrats.

An outspoken and fearless advocate for LGBTQ+ rights and an "unlikely" New Hampshire political mogul, he has demonstrated his leadership in a state that is 94 percent white.[15] And throughout his years of political engagement and leadership, he has been able to leverage the longstanding tradition of New Hampshire's first-in-the-nation primary to accrue an astounding amount of political power.

In the run-up to New Hampshire's February 11, 2020 vote, Carlos has single-handedly brought fifteen presidential candidates to his hometown—nine of those visitors held their meet-and-greet parties at his family's personal home.[16]

---

15   "New Hampshire Quick Facts," United States Census Bureau, accessed September 28, 2020.

16   Bill Donahue, "The Startling Political Power of One New Hampshire Resident," *Washington Post*, August 1, 2019.

Presidential hopefuls like Andrew Yang, Elizabeth Warren, and Bernie Sanders have visited Carlos' eight-bedroom lavender-colored home in Laconia near the glittering waters of the Opechee Bay where he lives with both his and his partner's mother, as well as one of Carlos' brothers.

Hundreds have gathered on his grassy front yard alongside Carlos' partner of thirteen years, John Swain, and his four-year-old daughter Sofia. Both Sofia and their soon-to-be one-year old son certainly have a lot to look forward to.

CHAPTER 14

MARTY MARTINEZ

———

On April 17, 2018, Marty Martinez boarded Southwest Airlines flight #1380 from New York City's LaGuardia Airport to Dallas, Texas. He had boarded hundreds of flights just like this one, and he didn't expect it to be much different than the flights he had boarded in the past. However, the flight that he was about to board—unbeknownst to him—changed the trajectory of his entire life.

About twenty minutes into the four-hour flight to Dallas, Marty faced the reality that his life, along with the lives of the other 143 passengers aboard, were in real danger.

One of the plane's windows had gone out after the explosion of the engine. This caused total destabilization of the plane and the depressurization on the plane triggered the oxygen masks to descend from above.

This could only mean one thing: the plane was above 15,000 feet in elevation from the ground for folks on board.

In the rush of the moment, Marty scrambled to open his laptop. The thought of losing his life without saying his final goodbyes to his loved ones was a thought he most certainly couldn't bear. He frantically typed his credit card number in and was able to access the in-flight Wi-Fi.

Now, he had to face the difficult decision of whom he would reach out to and what he would say to those loved ones. This was too painful to consider and in the rush of the moment, he opted for a Facebook Live.

"Brace yourself," someone yelled.

As Marty began the Facebook Live and started describing what was happening around him, he pointed the camera at himself breathing through the oxygen masks. Breathing in and breathing out. Sitting in the window seat, helpless. Unable to do much else except prepare himself for the worst.

Flight attendants desperately ran across the aircraft calling for passengers to help cover the hole that had been caused by the explosion of the engine. The desperation and anguish were almost palpable.

Then, Marty turned the camera to his fellow passengers. A sordid stillness overcame the airplane. A silence. A silence, an uncertainty, a fear of the unknown. Fear of fate. Fear of the future, of what might lay ahead for each and every single person aboard.

Suddenly, the plane dropped dramatically, and a pungent smell of fire started to overwhelm the environment.

Southwest 1380 had plunged 8,000 feet. Seats shook. A man sitting close to Marty's seat on the plane closed his eyes in prayer.

Within seconds, the silence suddenly ended as a woman who was seated three rows in front of Marty had half of her body sucked out of the open hole on the plane.

The reality sunk in. It could have been anyone. That could have been Marty.

And within the next five minutes, the aircraft descended heavily to approximately 11,000 feet above ground.

"Prepare for emergency landing," someone shouted.

Sitting in a window seat on the right wing of the plane, Marty couldn't believe his eyes. The plane was approaching a city.

Yet he couldn't recognize the city where the plane had landed. Was it Philadelphia?

A few more minutes after this, the plane finally landed.

Exactly ten minutes after the initial explosion, they were all finally safe. Some passengers were in complete utter silence, while others still showed signs of shock.

Alas, they had landed in Philadelphia and were safe and finally on the ground. A huge sense of relief embedded with feelings of fear, confusion, and anguish began to emerge.

For the passengers, their bodies were intact, but their minds certainly weren't. Marty, for one, couldn't bear to board another flight back to Dallas and rented a car to drive from Philadelphia to New York.

As he recounted the story to multiple news outlets who reported on the accident, the reality began to set in.

Why had he been spared? Why was he alive? For what purpose? It could have easily been his body that was partially sucked out of a window thousands of feet above ground. Yet, here he was, alive and well.

This event turned out to be a crossroads in Marty's life. In so many ways, it forced him to reflect on his life's purpose, to think about what he would do with the rest of the time he had on Earth.

Marty would soon be finding those answers within himself. Although this harrowing event marked a critical point in Marty's journey, his trajectory began long before that day in 2018.

Marty's journey began in Kansas City, Missouri. Growing up, encouragement and the belief in Marty's potential for success were the last things that were lacking in his household. His upbringing was marvelously filled with positive reinforcements and continuous and indomitable support from his parents, particularly his mother. However, this wasn't the case outside of his home, and Marty would have to face that head-on at such a young age.

In 2003, at just thirteen years old, Marty understood that he didn't want to take the path that many members of his family and community had taken.

The truth was this:

More people went to prison in his family than graduated college, but deep-down Marty knew that he was meant for something different, for a different life, and a different path.

So, when he aged out of the college prep school that he had been attending, he begged his parents to move out of their humble, working-class neighborhood to a more affluent, "white" neighborhood, so Marty could have the opportunity to attend the well-resourced and well-funded high school that would correspond to the area.

Marty knew that his environment would end up being a huge indicator of his trajectory later on. His parents agreed with their son and took out a large loan that at the time they couldn't afford but, in reality, what they couldn't really afford was to not support their son in his dreams of becoming more than they could ever be.

And Marty definitely became the man that his family and he once dreamed that he would be. He became the first in his family to graduate from high school and the first in his family to graduate from college. His work was cut out for him and the journey had really just begun.

After college, in hopes of having access to better opportunities, Marty moved to Dallas, Texas. The journey didn't include an easy start; he didn't know a soul in his new city and moving there proved to be quite the challenge. After having worked for a winery and a startup, he embarked on a journey to start his own company, now one of the most successful PR agencies in Texas—Social Revolt.

Right about this time in Marty's journey, he began to wrestle with his identity as a Latino. At the age of twenty-five, he didn't know a single successful Latinx. That is, until he attended an event for Latinx executives in the tech world. Only then did he realize that he wasn't alone. That there were in fact, many Latinxs, just like him, who shared similar backgrounds and similar dreams and aspirations.

One man in particular, at this event, approached him.

"Here's my card. Let's keep in touch." he said after a few minutes of conversation.

"After this, contact me and we'll get to know each other," he added.

This man, Andre Arbalez, would soon become an instrumental mentor and influence in Marty's career. Marty had a good feeling about this.

In fact, meeting Andre would prove to be the catalyst for Marty's personal journey to embrace his identity and his connection to the Latinx community at large.

During this chapter of his journey, Marty realized that because he hadn't been embracing his Latinx identity, he had in fact been operating with a handicap. After coming to terms with this, he realized that he was no longer willing to put up with that and deprive himself of the opportunity of flourishing, not despite his Latinx identity, but *because of it.*

What Marty thought was his biggest weakness is his biggest strength today. His Latinidad is what makes him resilient. It's what makes him powerful. The way that he sees it, it's the reason why he'll never be out-worked or out-hustled.

In fact, in his eyes, being Latinx is an unfair advantage to his white counterparts.

This realization and embrace of this part of his identity would bring about some of the most incredible and notable experiences Marty would have to date.

In December 2019, after years of incessant hustling and building the foundation of his agency, and a year after the tragic accident on the Southwest Airlines flight, Marty decided that it was finally time for a break. He booked a flight and decided to hop on a plane for an impromptu trip to Switzerland, no less. He didn't tell anyone and left the country for what should have been a two-week stay.

After arriving in the Swiss Alps and going on what would be his second time skiing, he calmly and intentionally sat down to write.

Amid the stillness of the air and the crisp oxygen that penetrated his lungs, he began to let his thoughts begin to roam.

He started to feel and grasp what he had been longing for and what this trip was meant for: to be in touch with himself. Little did he know, the universe had something exquisite coming his way.

He received a message from Andre.

"I don't want to bother you, but please when you have a moment—call me."

Andre knew just how vital this trip was for Marty and knew that if Andre was reaching out, it had to be important.

"Claudia Romo Edelman wants you to call her," Andre said through the phone. Marty took a deep breath unsure of where this was all going.

Claudia Romo Edelman is a world-renowned social entrepreneur, diplomat, and a remarkable advocate for equity, inclusion, and representation. She is the former chief of advocacy of UNICEF, current Special Advisor at the United Nations, and founder of the We Are All Human Foundation. Marty and Claudia had met a couple of times in New York before this, but that didn't prevent him from feeling absolutely petrified of calling her.

A call with someone as well-known and well-respected as Claudia certainly merits this kind of response. And as is expected, Marty got around to making that call.

An upbeat start, no less, with an unexpected twist.

"Marty, I know you've been on vacation for a minute now, but I don't know if you would be interested in joining us at the World Economic Forum's very first US Hispanic Delegation," Claudia confidently said.

"I think you'd be great," she added.

Marty's heart dropped. He didn't have the slightest idea that he was on Claudia's radar for an opportunity this grand.

The World Economic Forum in Davos, Switzerland is attended by some of the most influential leaders from around the globe. Nearly three thousand participants from 117 different countries were expected to attend. Imagine the world's most powerful and influential leaders from politics, business, civil society, academia, media, and the arts.

Such a remarkable and historic opportunity was impossible to turn down. The Hispanic Delegation included: Raquel Tamez, CEO, Society of Hispanic Professional Engineers; Miguel Alemany, Chair of the Board, Society of Hispanic Professional Engineers; Jesse Martinez, Founder, Latino Startup Alliance; Dr. Robert Rodriguez, President, DRR Advisors; and of course, Marty.

There's no way I can afford this, Marty thought to himself. He had already planned two weeks in Switzerland, and this would extend that stay even longer. Surely, a trip to an event that is attended by six hundred of the world's billionaires would not be economically effective.

If there's one thing that we can always count on as Latinxs, it's the ability of finding a way and making it happen. And Marty did just that.

Their presence, at Davos, was a true testament of how the global business community is beginning to grasp just how important and vital US Latinxs are for their success. And more than that, it's a testament to Marty's unlimited potential as the next face of influence that transcends far past US borders.

CHAPTER 15

YADIRA SANCHEZ

———

"Today we march, tomorrow we vote."

One-hundred-thirty cities. Thirty-nine different states.

In 2006, hundreds of thousands of people protested against a bill—which, among other provisions, would have criminalized assistance to undocumented immigrants who were seeking food, housing, and medical attention—proposed by US Representative F. James Sensenbrenner Jr., a Republican from Wisconsin.

H.R. 4437, informally called the Sensenbrenner bill, proposed to raise penalties for so-called "illegal immigration" and classify undocumented immigrants and any individuals who helped them enter or remain in the United States as felons.

Latinxs not only protested against the bill but also advocated for a comprehensive and just reform of this country's immigration laws that specifically included a path to citizenship for all twelve million undocumented immigrants living in the United States.

These robust mobilizations are seen today as a historic turning point for Latinxs in US politics and a catalyst for Latinx immigrant civic participation as well as the exertion of political influence. The Latinx community stayed true to their vow of taking matters into their own hands at the ballot box, and they did so by bringing unprecedented victory to Democratic candidates in an overtly apparent rejection of the Republican party's efforts to blame a tremendous amount of the nation's problems on immigrants.

What's more is that many of the young people who attended these marches had their first taste of political power at these demonstrations. Yadira Sanchez was one of them.

When Yadira Sanchez was eighteen years old and a first-year student at the University of California, Santa Barbara, she attended what would be the catalyst for an incredible career in Latinx civic empowerment—her very first protest in the fight for a just reformation of US immigration policy.

On a warm and mild spring day, she arrived at a meeting place just outside of an all-time favorite and go-to place for UCSB students right in the heart of the downtown area. As she began to walk towards the crowd of Black and Brown students who had gathered outside of the front of the building, she was surprised to see both familiar and unfamiliar faces in the crowd.

Now formally a Hispanic Serving Institution, UCSB has had a rich history in Chicanx and Latinx student organizations. When she arrived at the meeting place, Yadira saw classmates who were involved with Mujeres Unidas por Justice,

Educación y Revolución (M.U.J.E.R) as well as a number of Latinx fraternities and sororities.

However, when she looked to the other side of the narrow street, she saw something rather unexpected. A group of anti-protesters had congregated along the other side of the road.

"If you don't like it, then go back to your country," she heard one of them yell.

This would be the first of many times that Yadira would hear someone yell those words. Shocked and disconcerted to see the presence of anti-protesters, she took a moment to reflect on their faces.

Wearing ponchos and sombreros, they grunted and booed at the crowd of protesters. These were white students—your classic "California bros", if you will—wearing shorts and flip-flops inciting hateful and disturbing sentiments.

Yadira looked at them and thought about where she had seen them before. Surely, there was no way that Yadira hadn't run into them as they were all students on the UCSB campus. Suddenly, it hit her.

One of these young men or perhaps all of them had been seen at Freebirds, the go-to Mexican restaurant that the group of protesters chose for their meeting place.

"They eat our food, enjoy our culture, but hate our people," Yadira thought to herself.

She noticed that one of the anti-protesters was specifically yelling at one of her friends in the crowd.

"It's not worth it," she heard another student yell serenely as they continued on walking.

"They want us to get in trouble," he noted.

Her friend listened and backed off. You could feel the rage in his body, the indignation on his face.

Alas, they continued. One foot in front of the other.

"El pueblo unido jamás será vencido."

"El pueblo unido jamás será vencido."

Yadira looked behind her, to take one good look at *su gente* and recognized her university's cooks, dishwashers, and other staff from the university. This ignited a fire within her.

Everyone was walking on one unified beat, homemade maracas composed of water jugs filled with unidentified objects and all. Hooting and hollering—they were being heard. And as they got closer and closer to the end of the hill, Yadira could smell the fragrance of the beach and hear the waves crashing at a distance.

Chants of "Sí se puede" seemed to bounce off of all the lips of the people in the crowd.

Together—whether you were undocumented, documented, or simply born on American soil—you were together as one.

And this was just the start for Yadira. Nobody could've imagined that just ten years later, the same young woman would be in the White House, no less, representing the voice of millions of Latinxs in the United States.

A week after the Supreme Court ruled on United States v. Texas in June of 2016, Yadira Sanchez was invited to a meeting convening the nation's top advocacy organizations.

On June 23, 2016, the Supreme Court of the United States announced it had deadlocked in a 4-4 decision challenging then-President Obama's immigration plan. The court affirmed a Fifth Circuit ruling halting Obama's 2014 executive action that allowed as many as five million unauthorized immigrants who were the parents of US citizens or lawful permanent residents to apply for a program that would spare them from deportation and provide work permits. The program was called Deferred Action for Parents of Americans and Law Permanent Residents plan, commonly referred to as DAPA.

The executive action, taken by then-President Obama, was enacted after years of frustration with Republicans in Congress who had repeatedly refused to support bipartisan Senate legislation to update immigration laws. Essentially, a coalition of twenty-six states, led by the state of Texas, took no time to challenge the plan and accused President Obama of changing the rules and abusing the power of his office by circumventing Congress.

The decision from the Supreme Court was just nine words long:

"The judgment is affirmed by an equally-divided court."

The hopes of millions of undocumented immigrants and their families vehemently crushed by the mere existence of nine words.

"It is heartbreaking for the millions of immigrants who have made their lives here," said President Obama in a press conference.

"Congress is not going to be able to ignore America forever," the President continued.

"It's a not a matter of if; it's a matter of when. We get these spasms of politics around immigration and fearmongering, and then our traditions and our history and our better impulses kick in."

The Obama administration was reluctant to sit on their laurels so they convened a meeting with the top advocacy organizations in the country, one of them being Mi Familia Vota, where Yadira served as their director of development.

The meeting was led by four of the most powerful women—who also happened to be Latinas—in the Obama White House: Senior Deputy Director of Public Engagement Julie Chavez Rodriguez, Senior Associate Director of Public Engagement Ginette Magaña, Special Assistant to the President for Immigration Policy Felicia Escobar, and none other than the highest ranking Latina, Assistant to the President and Director of Domestic Policy and Council Cecilia Muñoz.

Yadira candidly remembers the energy in the room. The tone was serious—there was no doubt about that—but the power and influence around that table was daunting. Not only had there been a gathering of this massive brain trust, but there was also a sense of incredible responsibility for the opportunity to impact that they had in front of them. An impact that had the possibility to influence millions and now, several years later Yadira continues to stand by that same commitment.

Today, as the co-founder of Poder Latinx, Yadira continues to elevate and deepen the framework in order to build a nation-wide political wave where the Latinx community—in all of its diversity—plays a key role in the transformation of this country as indispensable decision-makers of the political process.

CHAPTER 16

CHRISTOPHER JAY CUEVAS

—

In June 2016, a few days after the Pulse shooting in Orlando, Florida, Christopher Jay Cuevas sat stoically in the living room of an Airbnb across from four different individuals they had never met before. Their hands were placed stiffly by their sides while their feet were placed firmly on the ground.

At first, the silence, hopelessness, and grief dominated every single centimeter of the room. The silence seemed to duplicate, even triple in size as the seconds passed by. Grave silence—the kind that destroys everything in its way.

"I can't go talk to someone about my needs." Christopher said, finally defeating the silence.

Feeling overcome with grief and anguish, both within and around—Christopher let out a prevailing truth.

"I'm in a place of trauma."

The words felt like the breaking of the ubiquitous chains, granting them freedom, except freedom felt empty, lonely, and tired of drowning in pain.

It was a feeling that almost every single person in the room shared as well.

Forty-nine lives had been lost. Fifty-three had been wounded the night of the shooting.

Not only was it the second worst mass shooting by a single gun person in US history, but it was also the second deadliest attack on US soil since the events of September 11, 2001.[17]

And it wasn't just on any night. The shooting took place on "Latin Night." The fifty lives that were taken were nearly half Puerto Rican and the other half was Cuban, Dominican, Ecuadorian, Mexican, Salvadorian, and Venezuelan.[18]

Some were Black. Some were undocumented. Over half were under the age of thirty and the youngest victim had just turned eighteen years old. It all felt so egregiously close to home, so inhumanely personal.

Most of the people in this particular room were simply strangers—strangers who came together. They were individuals who survived the attack and those who lost loved ones too.

---

17 Lizette Alvarez, "Orlando Gunman Attacks Gay Nightclub Leaving 50 Dead," *New York Times*, June 12, 2016.

18 Anagha Srikanth, "How people are remembering the Pulse nightclub shooting, four years later," *The Hill*, June 12, 2020.

Isabel, Felipe, Marco, and Ben Francisco—the four people who initially began as strangers—made Christopher feel heard, feel embraced without a single touch, and for a short fleeting moment, it felt as though the pain had subdued. Their spirit and being seemed to feel lighter as they spoke.

Christopher stared at the faces and souls that were listening, hoping for an answer and the resolution they knew deep down wouldn't come so easily. It wasn't a switch that they could flip.

"We hear you, we understand," they said calmly.

Through word of mouth, and randomly unsolicited Facebook messages, community members affected by the shooting began gathering in people's homes. They all pitched in what they could and sunk into the feeling of not feeling or being alone.

Folks congregated both in spirit and in person. A true healing circle.

People held one another. People dwelled in the shared sense of disconnection that permeated their beings due to the absence of those lives who had been lost.

Some laughed, remembering delicate joyful moments shared. Dancing, living, breathing—being unapologetically themselves. Grief looks differently for different people, doesn't it? This radiant projection of having to face grief and loss was illuminated by an overwhelming sense of gratitude for the connections that were shared and the ties that could never be severed.

Some cried, as the pain of the stark reality heightened the undeniable presence of hate. Some were overcome with grief and anguish that it felt almost impossible to imagine a day where the pain would ever subside.

I remember feeling my chest sink into my stomach as I listened attentively to Christopher describe that moment in time. You could hear it in their voice that what they were sharing with me changed them forever.

Christopher grew up in a rural immigrant community in Florida, without the presence of a vibrant queer and transgender community. So, when Christopher first moved to Orlando, they felt as though they had finally found something that they were longing for throughout their life: the beauty of being in community with other queer, non-binary, and transgender individuals.

Being in these spaces propelled Christopher to be the most authentic version of themselves and embrace the value and worth of every single individual that was part of this beautiful community. However, Christopher also realized that within these communities, there was a tremendous need for the consideration and inclusion of Brown and Black queer, non-binary, and transgender people specifically.

The truth was this:

In Central Florida there hadn't ever really been a space for Brown and Black queer, non-binary, and transgender people outside of a nightclub, outside of Pulse, where they could elevate those intersections and really come together.

There was no space created for empowering the local LGBTQ+ Latinx community to foster that growth and the healing—free from judgement and persecution in a way that was not shamed but embraced.

"Don't wait for other people to make that happen," someone said without an ounce of uncertainty.

Two weeks after that initial comment, the group gathered once again, this time at another home.

On this occasion, things took quite an interesting and equally surprising turn.

After snacking, chatting about how they were feeling, and later watching a movie—the group unabashedly switched it up.

"It's time to get to work," someone said.

"What work," Christopher remembers thinking. Christopher was almost certain that the comment about making things happen that was made the last time they got together wouldn't come up again. Or at least they hoped it wouldn't.

Oh, but it did, and it hit Christopher like a ton of bricks.

Christopher's realization of the fact that that comment was made in *earnest* was disruptive. They were in utter disbelief. There were no more awkward laughs, no more friendly expressions—this was it. Things were serious.

There's no way to describe that moment in time other than an unapologetic and fearlessly audacious order.

"It was like, wow, that was a great movie...and then BAM. Let's get to work." Christopher shared with warmth as they remember the moment vividly.

They were in awe of the sharp determination of everyone in the room.

As Christopher looked to gauge the others' expressions, they realized that the only person in that room who had been doubting their potential to lead was themself. So, as they sat in disbelief and admiration of others' initiative and grit, they found themselves wanting to believe. And so, they did. And so, it began.

QLatinx, a grassroots racial, social, and gender justice organization dedicated to the advancement and empowerment of Central Florida's LGBTQ+ Latinx community, was formed. With no one other than Christopher Jay Cuevas at the helm.

Christopher and the rest of the team began building supportive infrastructure, engaging community members directly, and providing a space for people to heal and to thrive.

A month later, Christopher was sitting in a conference room with Orlando Mayor Buddy Dyer, the first openly-gay elected official in Central Florida, City Councilmember Patty Sheehan, and Carlos Guillermo Smith, who would soon become the first openly LGBTQ+ Latinx person elected to the Florida State Legislature.

Christopher shared the plan QLatinx had developed to create and construct real pathways for the empowerment and healing for the local Latinx LGBTQ+ community.

It was in the middle of the workday and the rest of Christopher's team couldn't make it.

"Christopher, go."

"Christopher, I can't make it, but I trust you," one of their colleagues said to them.

They remember this unrelenting belief in their potential still making them feel uncomfortable. However, this time and ever since that day after the movie ended, Christopher has been diving deep into that discomfort and leading like no other.

Leading, like the leader they were always meant to be. They do so by working to honor the memory of those whose lives were taken. They do so by rewriting the narrative and garnering strength from the impact of hate. They do so by honoring and centering the work and mission of those who will hopefully never have to feel the impact of hate and fear again.

CHAPTER 17

REGINA MONGE

———

The furniture felt rather cold to the touch as Regina Monge stood barefoot on top of it. It was January in Washington and Regina wore a long sleeve crop top, a light sweater, and what were supposed to be her most comfortable pair of jeans.

After climbing her way up on top of the furniture, Regina, who stood there with a hammer in hand and unassailable determination, proceeded to nail a picture frame onto the wall.

"I remember thinking right as I was about to nail it onto the wall—are we even allowed to do this?" she said to me warmly.

The idea of permanently stabbing a nail onto *any wall* is terrifying. In fact, as I listened to Regina share this story with me, I realized that climbing onto furniture also sounded like a rather daunting thing to do in these circumstances. I couldn't even begin to fathom what it must have felt like physically for her to be doing this—especially in the place that she did.

That's because climbing onto furniture and nailing things onto walls takes on a whole new meaning when it's US Capitol furniture you're climbing on and the walls that you're penetrating are the walls that witness members of Congress make decisions that will affect the lives of thousands of Americans back home in their districts and, ultimately, in communities all over the country.

It was January 2019 and after months of working tirelessly as part of the finance team for a candidate whom she believed in and making history in electing the first South American immigrant to the US House of Representatives, Regina was asked to be part of the DC on-boarding team for the newly-elected and soon-to-be sworn in US Congresswoman Debbie Mucarsel-Powell.

Actions that seemed so ordinary and unpretentious now had a whole new meaning for Regina. Actions like vacuuming carpets and rearranging furniture, which could be considered so normal, now held a towering sense of power and importance to the entire staff that accompanied the future Congresswoman on this journey—but particularly to Regina.

Some might see it as the decoration and possible design of a brand-new congressional office. Perhaps the putting together of the bits pieces that made it come alive and more authentic to the people that she was serving. But, to Regina, there was so much more meaning, nuance, and depth to it.

I could feel it in her voice.

There was something about the actual physical labor of these actions during this time in her life that gave way to something so sacred.

As the proud granddaughter of carpenters, she never—in a million years—imagined that she'd have this full circle moment.

As she continued to complete the tasks, Regina's mind raced to times where physical labor presented such a complex set of emotions. Many years before this very day, Regina and her father got into a van and drove to DC to move Regina into her very first college dorm room at American University. As they moved Regina into her very first dorm, Regina's father was mistaken for a custodian by one of Regina's soon-to-be classmates.

Our conversation took a heavy turn as she revealed this part of the story.

"The girl that confused my dad for a custodian didn't even think anything of it," she said to me.

"She asked my dad to carry her belongings into her dorm room."

The silence between us both stung as if the very hammer that she was describing just moments before this was dropped in the most vulnerable of places.

I couldn't help it.

This part of her story struck a chord within me. A painful one, if I'm being honest. As I stood there listening to Regina's tone start to change as she shared this part of her journey with me, I could hear waves of pain and anger so subtly start to form in her voice. It was the kind of anger and pain that is transmitted from one person to another ever so easily, ever so rapidly.

My chest started to tighten, and I could feel my stomach start to twist inside me.

The emotions, for me, dragged out long after I finished my conversation with Regina that day. In fact, it's those very emotions that made this chapter the hardest in this book to write.

At first, I didn't really understand the depth of the emotions that were elicited when this was shared with me. I knew it certainly wasn't just rage caused by an inconsiderate, thoughtless error made by someone who simply didn't know any better.

In so many ways, I was not only enraged at the fact that this person would ever confuse someone's immigrant-looking and immigrant-sounding father for a custodian but I was also enraged with myself. Why would I feel denigrated by the fact that someone might confuse my father or anybody's parent for a custodian?

What was ever so denigrating about a person who made their living and put a roof over their family's head by using their hands?

Why would I take offense to it?

Taking offense to it would mean that I was promoting anti-working class, elitist sentiments. It's at this time when

I realized that the reason why I was feeling so triggered was because I had accepted those notions in my past. I had felt shame about my working-class parents for the better part of my childhood. I, too, had fallen victim to these narratives and imposed the shame onto myself and the pain onto my family.

While it's been so incredibly painful to heal from the shame that I once felt and transmitted to the people I love most in this world, what has been most transformative has been finding the strength in forgiving that six-year-old Claudia that ran to her parents' car after school as fast as she could so her classmates wouldn't have to see her family's old car.

It's the strength that it took to forgive that twelve-year-old little girl that begged her parents to dress more nicely to Parents' Back-to-School night just so nobody would know that we weren't as well off as all my classmates.

These memories will, for better or worse, always stay with me but it's the realization that those hands, those working hands—sometimes rough to the touch, always close to the heart, that make every single victory, every single step along the journey that much more profound, meaningful, and transformative.

CONCLUSION

In order to know what power looks like within yourself, you have to had to felt *powerlessness*. You've had to experience the utter disregard, the blatant underestimation, and the brazen apathy. You've had to experience the ravishing desire of those debilitating thoughts trying to permeate your system—wanting for you to believe that this state is permanent and not temporary.

For far too long, Latinxs—both young and old—in this country have been underestimated, overlooked, and underserved. The narrative has always been focused on the hardships, the struggles, and the inequities. While those inequities still very much exist and are hard-hitting realities for many regardless of your generation, there is something so incredibly transformative in the way that Millennial and Gen Z Latinxs are utilizing these limiting frameworks to catapult them and their communities into greatness.

They are firmly and unequivocally rejecting these limiting and denigrating assertions by utilizing them as fuel to propel them forward like never before.

I hope this book, no matter what your background, age, or political beliefs, has helped you understand that there has never been a more perfect time to unleash, elevate, and recognize the limitless power that young Latinxs hold in this country.

The better we do it, the better we'll be.

ACKNOWLEDGEMENTS

This endeavor wouldn't have been made possible without the generous support of some incredible people from all different chapters of my life. From people who have witnessed my journey since I was a little girl, to my teachers in high school, to beautiful people from my college days at Villanova, to my very best friends, to my beloved family, to some of the most amazing individuals I've had the pleasure of meeting in DC, and to some remarkable people I have yet to meet in person—each and every one of you has made this possible.

This, too, is yours.

Thank you for seeing something in me, believing in this book, and for making this dream a reality.

Flavia Alarco Mavila & Carlos Alarco Breña
The Verduguez Ordinola Family
Jacqueline Diaz-Mewes

Rebecca Bruckenstein
Elisabett Rico
Catherine Hunter
The Office of the President at Villanova University
Ingrid & Catherine Pino Duran
Mckenzee Chiam & Maura Lavelle
Nigel Sanchez
Meg & Jay Micou
Adriana Campos-Korn
Chris Melody Fields
Jerold J. Samet
Elena Mavila Galván & Salvador Valenzuela
Hugo Alarco Delgado & Flora Narrea
Vanessa & Kristel Herrera Noriega
Elsa Noriega Mavila
Ana Breña Mavila
Danielle McIntee
Edgardo Ortiz Diaz
Courtney Duncan
Isabella Sanchez Castañeda
Alejandro Roark
José Ignacio Gaona
Catalina Rodriguez Tapia
Mary Anna Ebbert
Jaison Binns
Yeralmi Massiel Vallardes
Karen Suzuki
Sara van Geertruyden
Jack Skaggs
Juliana Downey
Maria Martinez
Piero Vasquez & Gloria Campos

Liz Roukis
Lenny de la Rosa
Christina Kiedrow
Jacqueline Doddy
Lilibeth Mata
Denzell Stanislaus
Karina Castillo
Kevin McClintock-Batista
Cameron Cook
Justin Golding
Marifer Zacarias & Tomás Kloosterman
Chloe Wang
Jordan Newmark
Eric Koester
Angelica Serrano
Sheila Cato
Dr. Robert Rodriguez
Ivelisse Porroa
Diana Martinez
Elma McKinney
Sachi Kamiya
Joi Ridley
Sonia Benperlas
Diana Mejia
Malena Llanos
Kevin Saucedo-Broach
Ana Isabel Martinez Chamorro
Susan Pulongbarit
Crystal Young
Rina Grimaldi
Cindy Loveland
Margarita Sotelo

Maria Crupi
Taylor Hinch
Sophia Stanley
Suzette Phillips
Gemma Weightman
Jhael Calderón
Roberto Vásquez Alarco
Lorena Vásquez Villar
Keny Alarco Mendoza
Luis Alarco Breña & Paola Mendoza Navarro
Paul Sandro Alarco Breña
Luis Alarco Mendoza
Josué Ambriz
Claudia Marconi
Ricardo Martinez
Blanchi Roblero
Alejandra Escobar Serrano
Matthew Plucienik
Jalissa Madrid
Laura McGuigan
Ashley Boren
Alicia Valdez
Melanie Outtarac
Robert Hughes
Rebecca DeLorenzo
Michelle Moore
Iván Gonzalez Ayala
Arely Ramirez-Diaz
Randy Palacios
Paulina Vera
Liam Cafferty
Audrey Dunsmore

Cosmina Visan
Jeanette Ceja
Oscar Ramirez
Nora Manosca
Isaiah Alicea

INTERVIEWEE ACKNOWLEDGEMENTS

—

This book simply would not be possible without your candor, your trust, and your willingness to share your story with the world. Todo el respeto y el cariño para cada uno de ustedes.

MARISOL SAMAYOA
SHE/HER/ELLA

Marisol Samayoa is a bilingual communications professional who has worked for top Democratic candidates running for office at all levels of government from president to mayor. Most recently, she served as the deputy communications director and Hispanic media advisor for Mark Kelly's campaign for US Senate in Arizona. Marisol is a graduate of California State University, Long Beach, and a native of Boyle Heights, California.

STEPHANIE OLARTE
SHE/HER/ELLA

Stephanie Olarte is a community organizer; she was born in Rhode Island is a first-generation American, her family migrated from Colombia. She recently founded CaneiWalk, an organization that focus on youth with disabilities that hopes to provide them with tools necessary to succeed and empower them to live independently and achieve a higher education. Stephanie also founded a consulting firm Step Forward Strategies; this firm is unapologetic about its love for Latinx, other BIPOCs and disabled people, and the movement to create a more diverse and inclusive space in politics, social campaigns and in the workforce.

PAULINA MONTAÑEZ-MONTES
SHE/HER/ELLA

Paulina has spent nearly a decade serving as an advisor and operative in both local and federal government and on campaigns; currently, she is the Digital Strategist for Protect Democracy, a non-profit, nonpartisan organization dedicated to preventing American democracy from declining into a more authoritarian form of government. Prior to that, she led fundraising efforts for a number of successful high-profile Congressional races at a boutique digital firm. She also served as a political appointee for the Obama administration in Secretary Penny Pritzker's office at the US Department of Commerce. Paulina earned her bachelor's degree from the University of California, San Diego and her master's degree from the George Washington University.

EDGAR GONZALEZ, JR.
HE/HIM/HIS

Edgar Gonzalez, Jr. is the state representative of Illinois's 21st House district, a predominantly Latinx district. Edgar was born and raised in Chicago's Little Village neighborhood and was a member of Congressman Jesus "Chuy" Garcia's in-district constituent services staff before becoming state representative. Edgar is the son of immigrants from Monterrey, Nuevo Leon, Mexico. He graduated from the Harvard University in 2019 with a bachelor's in government.

JONATHAN FLORES
HE/HIM/EL

Jonathan is a first-generation US American, son of immigrants, and combat veteran. Since his deployment to Afghanistan, he's dedicated his life to seeking systemic change to defeat racism, mass incarceration, and imperialism. He's been part of multiple Americorps programs such as Teach for America and Public Allies and has most recently worked as the Latino constituency organizer for the Texas Democratic Party. This is only the beginning of the fight for the liberation of Black, Brown, and Indigenous communities.

KEVIN SAUCEDO-BROACH
HE/HIM/HIS

Kevin Saucedo-Broach is a Democratic activist and senior legislative aide working in the Virginia House of Delegates. One of ten siblings, Kevin was motivated by his background as the queer son of an undocumented father from Peru and a poor American mother to become a political advocate for social and economic justice. He lives in his hometown of Arlington, Virginia.

DIOMARA DELVALLE
SHE/HER/HERS

DioMara is a singer/songwriter from Brooklyn, NY who has also co-founded Million Watts, an entity led by artists, for artists. She recently released her EP, Alchemy, which is a testament to her transformational journey as a Black woman and her ability to see the divinity in who she is, as she is. DioMara has had the pleasure of sharing her talents and collaborating with entities such as BET, Afropunk, People Chica, Global Citizen, Facebook and so much more. She is bringing a voice to the multifaceted artist and with ownership and the cultivation of the Black community in mind, DioMara seeks to contribute to the ideal world we want to experience.

KEVIN LIMA
HE/HIM/HIS

Kevin Lima is the youth political director for the Democratic National Convention. Kevin leads youth engagement inside and outside of the DNC and helped build the youth infrastructure to help Democrats win key races across the country while simultaneously developing a diverse leadership pipeline to strengthen the future of the Democratic Party. Kevin has been a progressive political organizer since graduating with a political science degree from The Pennsylvania State University in 2016. He was an organizer for the Nevada State Coordinated Campaign in Las Vegas where he organized to elect the first Latina senator, Catherine Cortez Masto and worked for NextGen America as their CA campus and organizing director for the 2018 midterm.

MARIZOL LEYVA
SHE/HER/HERS

Marizol Leyva is a transgender model, author, cook, podcast host, and activist from the Bronx, New York. She has been featured in publications such as Vogue México, Cosmopolitan, Latina Magazine, Time Magazine's Motto, and People Magazine's Latina Love Project Series. She also has a podcast called Marizol Speaks. You can follow her on social media @iam_marizol for all of her latest projects.

DASH HARRIS
SHE/HER/ELLA

Dash Harris Machado is the co-founder of AfroLatino Travel, an organization that facilitates trips focused on centering Latin America's African roots, and co-host of the Radio Caña Negra podcast. A lifelong activist, she regularly hosts workshops designed to dismantle anti-Blackness, and in 2010, she produced NEGRO, a docu-series about the Latinx Identity and its deep-seated race, color, and class complex.

ANTONIO ARELLANO
HE/HIM/ÉL

Antonio Arellano is a human rights advocate and has been nationally recognized as one of the most influential Latinos in the United States by Hispanicize. As interim executive director of Jolt, Antonio is a catalyst for change in Texas. He is a proven fighter, whose efforts have resulted in the engagement, mobilization, and participation of thousands of young Latino voters.

CARLOS CARDONA
HE/HIM/HIS

Carlos was born in Aguadilla, PR. He is the Laconia Dems Chairman, Chairman of New Hampshire Progressive Coalition, and was the youngest elected official in 2007. He is currently working to get elected and represent Belknap District #3 Laconia NH.

MARTY MARTINEZ
HE/HIM/HIS

Marty Martinez is a founder and CEO of Social Revolt Agency, an award-winning marketing agency based in Dallas, Texas. Marty was also part of the first-ever Hispanic Delegation at the World Economic Forum in Davos, Switzerland where he met with global leaders to advocate for the importance of the Hispanic community to any businesses' growth strategy. As a son of immigrants, Marty is passionate about creating opportunities for the Latino community and dedicates much of his time to the Hispanic Star, a platform created to showcase and amplify the contributions of the Hispanic community to the United States, not only as an integral part of the American culture but also as an undeniable force shaping its future.

YADIRA SANCHEZ
SHE/HER/HERS

Yadira Sanchez is the co-executive director of Poder Latinx, a civic and social justice organization dedicated to building a political wave where Latinx communities, immigrants, and people of color are decision-makers in our democracy and in the transformation of our country. She also provides fundraising consulting services to nonprofits including Corazon Latino, a nonprofit organization that provides access to the Latino community to conservation, health and nature, equity, and environmental education programs and served as the development director for Mi Familia Vota, where she helped raise over $20 million and triple the number of strategic partnerships with major organizations and allies to increase year-round civic participation within the Latinx community.

CHRISTOPHER CUEVAS
THEY/THEM/THEIRS

A lifelong peace practitioner, educator, and community organizer, Christopher leads their work for cultural transformation by centering the unapologetic and unwavering power of radical love. In 2016, following the horrific massacre at the Pulse Nightclub in Orlando, Florida, Christopher co-founded and is the executive director emeritus of QLatinx, a racial, social, and gender justice movement working toward the advancement of intersecting LGBTQ+ Latinx issues. A child of undocumented immigrants and a queer person of color, Christopher interconnects their lived experience and drives the necessary heart work of building a culture of peace, compassion, and change through advocating for LGBTQ+, immigrant, and racial justice movements.

APPENDIX

———

AUTHOR'S NOTE

- Manning, Jennifer E. "Women in Congress: Statistics and Brief Overview." *Congressional Research Services* (January 2020): 2-10.

- Victory Institute. "Two LGBTQ Senators and Eight LGBTQ Representatives to Be Sworn In to Most Diverse Congress in U.S. History." Accessed September 13, 2020. https://victoryinstitute.org/news/lgbtq-members-116th-congress/

MARISOL SAMAYOA

- InnerCity Struggle. "Our Story: 25 Years of Eastside Movement Building." Accessed April 3, 2020. https://www.innercitystruggle.org/our_story

ALEJANDRO BARRAGÁN

- U.S. Department of Housing and Urban Development. "Julián Castro." Accessed July 22, 2020. https://archives.hud.gov/secretaries/castrobio.cfm

- Obama White House Archives. "Exit Memo: Department of Housing and Urban Development." Accessed July 29, 2020. https://obamawhitehouse.archives.gov/administration/cabinet/exit-memos/department-housing-urban-development

JONATHAN FLORES

- Farrell, Theo. "Unbeatable: Social Resources, Military Adaptation, and the Afghan Taliban." *Texas National Security Review* 1, no. 3 (May 2018):59-60.

- Farrell, Theo. "Unbeatable: Social Resources, Military Adaptation, and the Afghan Taliban." *Texas National Security Review* 1, no. 3 (May 2018):60-61.

KEVIN SAUCEDO-BROACH

- Nirappil, Fenit, "What Virginia's Governor-elect Ralph Northam (D) promised during his campaign." *Washington Post*, November 23, 2017. https://www.washingtonpost.com/local/virginia-politics/what-virginias-governor-elect-ralph-northam-d-promised-during-his-campaign/2017/11/23/a6a2dc4e-c992-11e7-8321-481fd63f174d_story.html

- Tackett, Michael, "In Virginia Governor's Race, Immigrants' Turnout May Be Key." *New York Times*, October 28, 2017. https://www.nytimes.com/2017/10/28/us/politics/virginia-governor-race-immigrants-northam-gillespie.html

MARIZOL LEYVA

- Smith, Morgan. "OITNB's Selenis Leyva: Working with Laverne Cox Helped Me Understand My Trans Sister's Journey." *People Magazine*, March 24, 2020. https://people.com/tv/oitnb-selenis-leyva-transgender-sister-marizol-leyva-book-laverne-cox/.

DASH HARRIS

- Refinery29. "No, I'm Not A Proud Latina." Accessed October 1, 2020. https://www.refinery29.com/en-us/latinx-identity-black-history-personal-essay

ANTONIO ARELLANO

- Zavaleta, Lourdes. "Man of Action." *OutSmart Magazine*, September 2019.

CARLOS CARDONA

- *BarackObamadotcom.* "Barack Obama Files for the New Hampshire Primary." October 25, 2007. Video, 1:53. https://www.youtube.com/watch?v=Tj8xwSOwO2s

- Nagourney, Adam. "Debate Preview: All Eyes on Obama." *New York Times*, October 30, 2007. https://thecaucus.blogs.nytimes.com/2007/10/30/debate-preview-all-eyes-on-obama/?mtrref=undefined&assetType=REGIWALL&mtrref=thecaucus.blogs.nytimes.com&assetType=PAYWALL

- United States Census Bureau. "New Hampshire Quick Facts." Accessed September 28, 2020. https://www.census.gov/quickfacts/NH

- Donahue, Bill. "The Startling Political Power of One New Hampshire Resident." *Washington Post*, August 1, 2019. https://www.washingtonpost.com/news/magazine/wp/2019/08/01/feature/the-startling-political-power-of-carlos-cardona/

CHRISTOPHER JAY CUEVAS

- Alvarez, Lizette. "Orlando Gunman Attacks Gay Nightclub Leaving 50 Dead." *New York Times*, June 12, 2016. https://www.nytimes.com/2016/06/13/us/orlando-nightclub-shooting.html

- Srikanth, Anagha. "How people are remembering the Pulse nightclub shooting, four years later." *The Hill*, June 12, 2020. https://thehill.com/changing-america/respect/diversity-inclusion/502537-how-people-are-remembering-the-pulse-nightclub